Out of the Woods

GIB WOOD

Out of the Woods
© 2022 Gib Wood

Paperback ISBN: 978-1-66782-332-4
eBook ISBN: 978-1-66782-333-1

CONTENTS

Introduction   1

My Story – Abridged   3

Creation Super-highway   14

The Love Dolt   30

11th Commandment   38

Forgiveness   47

Tithes and Offerings   57

God's Politics – Revisited   68

What Does it Mean to Believe?   81

Postscript   89

Introduction

I write this book for my family. Hopefully, my grandchildren will some-day read it, and on down the line.

This is not a children's book. It is written assuming that whoever reads this will be old enough to understand most of the concepts, and if not, old enough to research those concepts that they don't understand.

For some reason, God made it hard for me to express my thoughts and ideas on a one-on-one basis. Writing them down is much easier for me as my feelings and mental projections don't get in the way as often. As an empathetic person, I tend to shut down a conversation if I feel that I'm losing someone. When that happens, my self-consciousness kicks in and I'm done for. I'm not known for soldiering ahead in a conversation unless I have complete buy-in from the listener, and we all know how rare that is.

Aside from the last chapter, this book is a series of talks that I gave at the Morse Church. Some of you may have heard them, but whether you were *actually listening* is another story. Fortunately, Brian Dahms (pastor of Morse Church) allowed me to give these talks because I was an oddity to him. I was a former atheist who came at Christianity from a different per-spective; one that he was unfamiliar with, but one that also intrigued him. But then again, Brian was a different sort of pastor, as some of us know. I do give credit to Brian for allowing a new Christian to give these talks in his start-up church—most would not. I also give Brian credit for the name of this collection as it was his suggestion from many years ago.

All of these talks are about issues I had to work through to become a Christian and issues I struggled with once I became a Christian. I have gone through and edited the talks and made changes to any information that may have been out of date and included some family asides. Beyond that, they are the actual talks except for the final chapter on "belief".

So, there you have it. Read this with an open mind; a mind that is capable of seeing and understanding Truth but still able to hold room for mystery; because mystery, as it relates to God, is everywhere.

My Story - Abridged

"Back when I was a little boy…."
– Grandma Betty Lou

My mother used to say to me when I was very young, "back when I was a little boy…" While you might think it could create some gender confusion, I was young enough that it was comforting that my mother was "a little boy" and had a relatable experience, even though I soon enough realized she was pulling my little leg. While I knew that I was born a boy and not a little girl, I did, however, think I was born an atheist.

I couldn't remember a time when I believed in God. Even as a young child, I didn't believe in God. I remember going to church and thinking how weird it was. I'd go to school and learn all these facts and figures, but I went to church once a week and learned about this guy, Jesus, who died 2,000 years ago but was supposed to love me today—it just didn't make sense. It all just felt so weird and foreign to me. And the pictures of Jesus compounded the issue. For example, the picture of Jesus holding a lamb. He looked more like a "hippy" than the son of God ("Hippies" were a relatively new phenomenon when I was growing up in the '60's). And the photo of Jesus sitting around the campfire talking to little kids reeked of "stranger danger". To me, church was a social club and my parents picked a bad one as all my friends went to other, "better" churches. I just couldn't believe that the adults at church believed this stuff either. It was like the emperor's clothes; I just knew that someday their eyes would be opened, and they'd see this nonsense for what it was.

Then something happened that confirmed to me that there was no God. When I was nine, my Mom died of cancer.

I distinctly remember not being mad at God; it just confirmed to me that there was no God. I remember my Aunt Mary and me looking at Mom in her casket, and she said to me, "God has a reason for taking your Mom." She was lucky I was nine and not a teenager, because I remember thinking that is nonsense, but I said nothing and just nodded my head.

I also remember in Junior High, I was walking home from school with two friends who were catholic, and I told them that I didn't believe in God. You could have knocked them over with a feather. As soon as their slacked jaws could operate again, they told me that I had better keep my mouth shut about that kind of stuff or I'd "burn in hell". That episode didn't change my mind about God, but it did enlighten me on who I should tell my secret. And then later, in high school, I was taught the Theory of Evolution, and I knew then that I was right; God never existed, and science explained it all.

Throughout my life, I have several strong memories of people trying to share their faith with me; maybe it was because I would challenge them. But it seemed to me that they could never give me a good answer for why they believed. Sure, they had heart-felt beliefs, but when I pressed them, they could never give me concrete reasons, only personal and spiritual reasons. To me that just wasn't enough.

In high school we had an art teacher named Mr. Allen. He was 6'4", and a former golden gloves boxer who commanded a lot of respect. He was the faculty "enforcer." If any of the high school "toughs" started making trouble, Mr. Allen would be called in to straighten them out. He was also the faculty "Jesus freak." He was a "born again" Christian and was on fire for Jesus. He even had his own house church (back when I was growing up, "respectable" people went to denominational churches. People who went to non-denominational churches were "one of those Christians" and were thought to be a little different). At that time, you could actually talk about religion in school. He even had scriptural references up in his class. Of course, he had John 3:16. Anyway, it was very easy to get him going when it came to religion. Most of the guys would just be playing devil's advocate—not me. I couldn't believe that he *really* believed that stuff. He would share his faith with me and tried to explain why he believed but it didn't take. I just thought it was all nonsense. I do remember one thing he said though; he said, "Man has an innate desire to seek God." Well, not me. My only innate desire was to find out what compelled otherwise intelligent people to believe this stuff.

Later when I was a senior, I was on my first date with a girl named Lori. We were going to Fort Dodge to see a movie. Ft. Dodge was seventeen miles from my hometown of Webster City. We went there because Ft. Dodge had a cinemaplex—they had a theatre with two screens. Well, it was the middle of winter and it was cold, very cold—well below zero. I can't believe our parents let us go. Of course, my car broke down on the way back; it over-heated. Can you believe it; it over-heated! Here we are in the middle of nowhere because, in my infinite wisdom, I had taken a short cut. If it had been summer, I'm sure Lori would have thought I planned it. But now we were worried about freezing to death because we were broken down in front of a ramshackle farmhouse that looked uninhabited with the nearest farm at least half a mile down the road. You have to understand; ramshackle farmhouses were not the norm in northcentral Iowa. This is some of the best farm ground in the world, and most farmers were very proud of how their farms looked. But we gave it a try anyway. We got out of the car and knocked on the door. It's only ten o'clock on a Friday night and all the lights are off except for the rear yard light. However, the lights come on when we knock, and it was this young couple and they're happy to see us! They inform us that we were the third car this month to break down in front of their house and that they knew that God had led us to them. Yes… we had entered the "Twilight Zone".

You see, they were "born again" Christians and couldn't wait to share their faith with us. So, they invited us in and let us use the phone. Come to find out they were members of Mr. Allen's house church. Of course, they shared their faith with us and told us how it changed their lives. Finally, our ride showed up and we got out alive. It was quite a first date. This whole episode convinced me on nothing. It was just a funny story to tell my friends.

After winters like that, and one year at the University of Iowa (quite possibly the coldest campus on earth), I decided it might be a good idea to head south for college. So, I went to University of Texas and joined a fraternity. Fraternities, like most groups, have cliques, many of which had names. Our Fraternity was no exception. One of these cliques was a group of guys from San Antonio. I don't what it was about San Antonio, it must have been the water, but these guys were known as the Thumpers (aka Bible beaters). They would have Thursday Bible studies and sit around playing guitar and singing Kum Bah Yah. If you've seen *Animal House*, someone sitting around playing the guitar doesn't go over really well in a frat house. But, by and large, they were fun guys, so they were tolerated. One of the Thumpers, Matt Cassidy, actually tried to evangelize me; probably because I would engage him in discussions about religion. I couldn't *believe* that he would waste his college career being a Thumper. I couldn't comprehend why someone would do that.

Now, I was in a clique known as the "TVs". We were called that because we controlled the frat house TV and scheduled our classes around *All My Children* (don't laugh, someone we may all know, watched into her 40's). Besides, Austin was a great place for *All My Children* as the local station was a day behind and an hour earlier than the San Antonio station. Think about it; you could watch two hours every other day and not miss an episode—great for scheduling classes. Anyway… so here is a TV (me) asking a Thumper why he was wasting his college career. Do you see anything wrong with that picture? Were my priorities screwed up or what?!

However, Matt told me that college was the perfect time because when you got out of college you get caught up in your career and have less time to spend on your faith. Well, I didn't buy it, but Matt shared his faith with me anyway, but it didn't take. True to his comment, Matt pursued a career for a few years after getting out of college but later went to seminary. Today, Matt is the senior pastor of a large, non-denominational church in Austin.

You see, some very spiritual people had shared their faith with me, but I couldn't *just* believe, no matter how compelling the belief was. And Christianity is a pretty compelling belief; you get to live forever, and all you have to do is believe and trust in Jesus.

That all changed in 2001 when my wife, Kathy[1], in an effort to get me to attend church on a regular basis, convinced me to go this new Church that had a rock band. Okay, I know what you are thinking, "What were you doing going to church? You didn't believe in God." Well, I was a hypocrite; I had learned early in life who to tell and who not to tell. Strangers, acquaintances, or fellow skeptics were okay but not people that mattered because I felt like I was letting them down. Besides, going to Church was my tradition. Even though I didn't believe in God or Jesus, I thought Christianity, as I understood it at the time, taught good life lessons but these ideals were man-made. However, I would only go to Church if there wasn't something better going on, and quite often, sleeping was a better deal.

So, we visited this new church that met in a junior high school. Their goal was to church the un-churched of Johnson County. To that end, as you left the service, they had a table with a select group of books for people who were new to Christianity or were skeptics. Since I fell into the latter category, I picked up two books, *The Jesus I Never Knew* by Philip Yancy and *A Case for Christ* by Lee Strobel. I read Yancy's book first, but it did

---

1 Grandma Mimzy

nothing for me as it was spiritual in nature. Stobel's book was interesting to me because it tried to prove who Jesus was and the events that surrounded His resurrection. However, I still didn't believe in God or Creation, so how could I believe in Jesus?

A few months later, the same author Strobel came out with *A Case for Faith,* so I picked it up and read it. After reading Chapter 3, I can honestly say my life changed forever. This chapter was about the science behind Creation. Lee Strobel, a former atheist, was interviewing Walter Bradley, a professor of mechanical engineering from Texas A&M University who had his PhD in materials science from The University of Texas and had headed up A&M's Polymer Technology Center. In addition, Professor Bradley was a member of an elite group of scientists who studied the origins of life. Among this group, it was common knowledge that life did not begin here on earth; that the building blocks of life (the primordial ooze) did not exist on earth at that time and the earth was not old enough for life to form and evolve as evolutionists propose. Furthermore, even if there were primordial ooze available for amino acids to form, which are needed to make protein, these amino acids are highly reactive in an oxygen rich atmosphere and would have to line up in such a precise manner (without reacting with other material) that the odds of this happening "are so infinitesimal that the human mind cannot comprehend them." In the words of Dr. Bradley, "the odds for all practical purposes are zero. Even though some people who aren't educated in this field still believe life emerged by chance, scientists simply don't believe this anymore." Dr. Bradley went on to say that given all the facts, that the most logical and well-supported explanation for life is that we are the product of an intelligent designer (or creator).

To me, the implications of this were immediate and profound. For the first time in my life, the thought occurred to me that maybe we were created. And if we were created, what I had read about Jesus might be true.

For the next two years I read everything I could get my hands on about evolution vs. Creation, and the history, archeology, and evidence behind Jesus and the Bible. I read and re-read the Bible. I took <u>Alpha</u> (as a skeptic). Kathy and I even studied the Jewish roots of our faith so we could get a better understanding of Jesus and his teachings. I went from sleeping through one sermon a month to listening to two to three a day on Christian radio.

But what all this study showed me is that some aspects of the Christian faith are not knowable; you just have to trust what the Bible tells you. Also, I learned that God is not some kind of cosmic killjoy and that my life would change for the better if I became a Christian, not worse as I had always assumed. But more importantly, I found that the most important aspects, the foundational aspects of the Christian faith, are true and knowable! Scientifically, there is virtually no doubt that Creation is true, and that evolution created life is a myth, despite what the secular world tells you. In every scientific discipline, from the fossil record to genetics, the evidence for Creation far outweighs the evidence of evolution. The only reason this is not apparent to many scientists is that they are adherents to a belief system known as naturalism which states that everything must come from nature, regardless of the evidence. To this group of people, the theory of evolution is the cornerstone of their belief system. Hopefully, this will change as more scientists are becoming Socratic scientists and are following the evidence wherever it leads regardless of the theological implication. **It takes far more faith to believe in evolution than Creation.**

Additionally, archeology, history, textual criticism, and prophecy have shown me that the Bible is true and trustworthy, and that no other religious book or philosophy can make that claim. There is not a reputable historian today that doubts that Jesus was a real, historic person. And the direct and circumstantial evidence surrounding His death and resurrection is so overwhelming that I have no doubt that He rose from the dead. Because of this knowledge, I was able to accept the gift of grace given freely by God to all of us through His son, Jesus Christ!

As you hear (or read) this, you might be thinking, "Nice story but how does this apply to my life and my story?" I'm glad you asked that question because I'm going to tell you.

I'd like to answer with two verses. First is John 14:11: "*Believe me when I say that I am in the Father and the Father is in me; or at least believe on the evidence of the miracles themselves.*"

Jesus, by this verse, is letting us know that He knew that faith alone was not enough for some people. In fact, most people didn't believe Him until He proved it with His miracles and resurrection. For many of us, me included, our gap of skepticism is too great to be bridged by faith alone. It takes evidence and proof in order for us to narrow that gap so that it *can* be bridged by faith. So, if you're struggling with doubts or are skeptical about the claims of Christianity, then you owe it to yourselves to look at the evidence with an open mind.

Now for those of you who are believers, I'd like to read the next passage, John 4:23-24: "*Yet a time is coming and has now come when the true worshipers will worship the Father in spirit and truth, for they are the kind of worshipers the Father seeks. God is spirit, and his worshipers must worship in spirit and in truth.*"

Most of you here today who are believers came to Christ spiritually—it just made sense to you and you've always "just believed." What I think Jesus is saying, especially in the context of this verse, is that it's great to just believe but you also need to know that what you believe is true. For me, I came to Christ because of truth and I'm working towards spirituality. For many of you, you came to Christ from a spiritual basis and are (or should be) working towards the Truth of God.

Let me give three reasons why I think that this is important. First, for your own faith. Many of you know people who you thought were deeply committed Christians who have walked away from their faith. It's obvious that the foundation of their faith couldn't withstand whatever it was that made them question their faith. We all have doubts at times. Most of the time we are able to work through them. But there may come a time when your faith is shaken to its very core—to its foundation. If your faith is built on these foundational facts, then your faith has a solid foundation that is not easily shaken. For me, I fall back on these truths almost daily. I was an atheist for forty years and there are times when my old doubts rear their ugly head. Something innocuous can happen or be said, and my old doubts come flooding back. But I can take a deep breath and remember that I know for a fact that we are Created, that Jesus was a real person who was crucified, dead and buried, and that He rose from dead... and I'm okay. I know with certainty these are true in the literal sense, not just a hopeful belief.

Secondly, to help you in sharing your faith with others. I have always envied people who could "just believe"; those who have the "child-like" faith that Jesus talked about. But there are a lot a people, like me, who can't "just believe"; they're not able to suspend their secular belief system and believe regardless of how compelling the belief is. Most of the people I know outside of church (and many within) fit into this category. Think about it, if they knew it was true don't you think that they would be in Church? In my experience, if you can get to the root of the issue, it is that they don't believe that it is true!

Getting back to my earlier experiences, whenever I talked to people about their faith it went something like this: "Why do you believe this stuff?"

"Because I know deep down inside that it's true."

"But how do you really know that it's true?"

"Because I believe the Bible is the inspired word of God."

"So how do you know the Bible is true?"

"Because I've seen how it's changed my life and others."

"No, how do you know it's true?"

"I just know."

"So, it's true for you."

"No, it's true for everyone."

"But how do you know that?"

"Because the Bible…"

To me, and most skeptics, this is circular reasoning and only proves that the believer had an irrational faith.

But today when someone asks me about my beliefs, I tell them I believe because it is true, factually true. Now this may surprise the people I'm taking to (including Christians) but if you're confident in what you know to be true, then it is much easier, in my experience, to share this with people and much less threatening than sharing your feelings, especially for men. The goal is not to convince people, but to just plant the seed of doubt that they might question what they believe so that their God-given curiosity might take over. From there, it's up to them, and as the Apostle John puts it, "the Spirit of Truth".

Lastly, and probably the most important, you need to learn these truths so that you can teach your children, grandchildren, nieces or nephews, or any child over which you have influence. You see, rarely is this information taught in Sunday school or church. Why? I'm not sure, but it is not. It took me forty years to discover this information on my own when it could have been taught to me at Church!

Today, more than ever, kids need to be able to defend their faith. The world is antagonistic toward Christianity. Children are coming to this battle between their faith and secularism unarmed and are losing the battle. There is a statistic I've heard mentioned that over eighty percent of professing Christians entering college leave as non-believers. This is an amazing statistic that illustrates how woefully unprepared our children are. While some will come back to their faith later in life, many won't… so why take the chance?

For this reason and this reason alone, I hope that you will take the time and effort to learn the irrefutable truths that are the foundation of the Christian faith.

<u>Suggested Reading</u>

A Case for Faith by Lee Strobel

Creation Super-highway

Today we are going to explore Creation from both the scientific and theistic perspectives. Now, this whole effort would take many, many weeks but I've cut it down to one simple, easy to use three-hour lesson (ha ha). I call this talk the "Creation Super-Highway". It's a take-off on the "Information Super-Highway." I've used this silly metaphor of a super-highway for several reasons; one is that I've found that most people, like me, or I should say, like I used to be, are on the "gravel on-ramp" to the creation super-highway and don't really know much about this debate and many don't really care.

In Romans, (Romans 1:18-25) Paul said that only the foolish deny Creation and there was no excuse as it is "self-evident." Now if someone had told me *that* as an atheist, I would have dismissed Paul as being foolish. Because, to me, evolution was self-evident—man looks like ape, therefore, man must have evolved from apes. Besides, it was what we were taught in school, so it had to be right. This was obvious to me, and only "deluded, religious types" believed in creation.

Now, most of you here today know that I've seen the errors of my ways, not in spite of science but because of science. The scientific debate between creation and evolution is the reason I'm a Christian today! So, what I'm going to do today is give a brief explanation of each perspective, give the objections to each, and then give my opinion. Lastly, I'm going to explain why this debate is so important.

As you can see from the chart below, there are four main theories as to how life began. Three of them have to do with a creator/or designer, and one denies the need for a creator. So, you have on the right two lanes, Creation Science and Intelligent Design (ID), and on the left lanes, theistic evolution and evolution.

Creation Super Highway

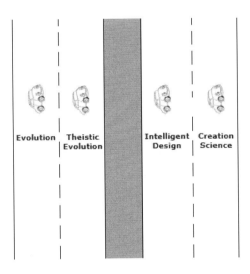

I'm going to let you in on a little secret; only one of these, in my opinion, is purely scientifically based. The others are tainted, to some degree, by religion with two manipulating science to fit their religion and one manipulating their religion to fit science. This may give it away but if you notice, the two cars in the right lane are heading in the correct direction, while the cars on the left are going the wrong way.

Ok, let's start with Creation Science. Most Creation scientists believe in a literal translation of the first eleven chapters of Genesis, that the earth and the universe are approximately 6,000-8,000 years old based on the genealogies contained in the Bible. They believe in a literal six days of creation. Further, they believe that most of the geological structures can be and are better explained by the worldwide flood that happened at the time of Noah. Now in case you think that people who hold this view are somehow incapable of intelligent thought, you may be surprised to learn that there are many, highly intelligent, PhD level scientists who hold to this argument, and they have some very persuasive arguments. Brian's dad, himself a chemical engineer and former president of an oil company, viewed many of their arguments as more rational than those views held by mainstream scientists.

Next, we have Intelligent Design. Many in the scientific community try to lump Intelligent Design into the category of "creation science." But it is distinct for a number of reasons, primarily as it is not an attempt to reconcile the Bible to science. Essentially, Intelligent Design is a scientific study to detect design within the natural world, much like anthropologists try to detect human activity from natural activity, or forensic scientists try to detect a causal activity from random activity. Further, ID holds that "certain features of the universe and living things are best explained by an intelligent cause rather than an undirected process such as natural selection."

Now let me back up for just a minute. There are three general types of scientists; first we have naturalists; they hold that everything must have a natural (or material) explanation regardless of the evidence. The vast majority of mainstream scientists today are naturalists. Second, we have Creation scientists, who hold that the Bible is the ultimate authority on Creation, and like naturalists, view science through their worldview. Lastly, we have Socratic scientists (taken from Plato's Socrates) who "follow the evidence wherever it leads" regardless of the implications. And this is the segment that most ID proponents find themselves in.

Now let's move to the left-hand lanes. First, we have theistic evolution, which essentially states the evolution is true, that it has occurred randomly but in some sense God has superintended this "random" process.

And lastly, we have evolution, which states the life began by chance and that it evolved over time through random mutations and the process of natural selection. Today, technically, evolution is known as neo-Darwinian Theory or Synthesis due to scientific evidence that has invalidated several aspects of Darwin's original Theory. For example, the theory of "punctuated equilibrium" came about in an attempt to explain the sudden influxes of life that appeared in the Cambrian era which go against Darwin's view of successive, gradual changes. Punctuated equilibrium has subsequently been discredited.

Now, what are the objections to each one of these theories?

First, with Creation Science, it is viewed as being biased. That it tries to manipulate science to fit a predetermined outcome. In addition, it is said to disregard well-established scientific data to arrive at its conclusion. Furthermore, many Christians say it harms evangelism because of that very fact. The argument goes that the Gospel is hard enough for non-believers to accept and it makes it even harder if they have to believe an esoteric scientific theory. Their argument goes on to state that you should not debate the age of the earth but emphasize the creation story contained in John 1:1-3: *In the beginning was the Word, and the Word was with God, and the Word was God. The Word was with God in the beginning. All things were created by him, and apart from him not one thing was created that has been created.*

With Intelligent Design, its critics say that it is not science because it is not falsifiable and therefore cannot be validated. And that it is just a new version of creation science but packaged better. That it is thinly veiled religion packaged as science because it implies a creator or god. Further, as ruled by a Pennsylvania judge, it is not science because most scientists say it is not science. I call this the "take your ball and go home" school of thought. Post modernism is alive and well in the scientific community.

Theistic Evolution. Its critics point out that it is a contradiction in terms. You cannot have a random process controlled by God. The very fact that God controls it eliminates randomness and makes it a structured process. Further, they point out that theistic evolutionists prefer the Theory of Evolution, because they can manipulate their theology to fit science; if man is evolving, then societies must be evolving and therefore, the gospel has to evolve to fit a changing humankind. Consequently, they can reshape the gospel to their image, instead of God's.

The critics of evolution attack it from several fronts. First, they point out that evolution is really two theories instead of one unified theory; that it is made up of microevolution and macroevolution. Microevolution is what Darwin proved, and it is a scientific fact that species adapt and change within the species. However, Darwin erred by extrapolating microevolution into macroevolution, by saying that species adapt and change into new species. Further, they point out that in every scientific discipline, the evidence for design far outweighs the evidence for evolution. That in fact, there is no hard evidence for macroevolution, only soft or visual evidence, i.e., man looks like ape, therefore, he must have evolved from apes. Lastly, they point out that Darwinian scientists are biased. That by stating that everything must have a natural explanation regardless of where the evidence leads, that they are arbitrary; that they are setting up these arbitrary limits to prop up their own religion or worldview, which is naturalism (or another name for it is Ontological Materialism, which is that all things come from matter and that there is nothing else but matter or material). Because of this, they give evolution a pass, scientifically, because, as with theistic evolutionists, it is the lynchpin of their belief system.

Okay, from here on out, I am going to give you my take on these differing views for the explanation of life.

First, I tend to agree with the critics of Creation Science. To me, the evidence for a young Earth, while interesting is less convincing than evidence for an earth that is several billion years old. Further, I see nothing in the Bible that doesn't harmonize well with an older dating of the earth and universe. To me, the creation story is about who and why, not how. With that being said, what scientists now know about the beginning of the earth and universe lines up amazing well with the cosmological events contained in Genesis. Further, the Hebrew word used for "day", yom, can mean either a specific day as in "Yom Kippur" or an "age" as in an era. It all depends on the context. So, each "age" lines up with the sequence of cosmological events that science now believes as factual. Additionally, the ancient Hebrews were the only ones who had their creation story correct, cosmologically. I also agree that it makes it harder for non-believers to believe if creation science is used as an evangelical tool. I certainly don't have any qualms about talking about creation but saying the creation happened in six days, 6,000 years ago is a definite conversation stopper for most people. Even if I could be convinced that it was a valid argument, I would not mention it when talking to unbelievers because of the implications and connotations of this argument.

I think you can probably see by now that I am a proponent of Intelligent Design (ID). From my research, it is the only purely scientific discipline of those I've mentioned. Despite what its critics say, ID is certainly falsifiable and offers far superior explanations for what we see in nature. For example, the skeletal structure of an antelope looks incredibly similar to that of a whale. Now, the evolutionist will say that it is obvious the antelope evolved from whale due to its similar skeletal structure. While there is absolutely no evidence other than this visual evidence, naturalist will completely disregard the obvious answer because it doesn't fit the prior commitment to naturalism. The answer that best explains this situation is that the designer of the whale and antelope used a common platform. It is an elementary and basic engineering principle that you don't re-engineer something that already works and serves the purpose for which it was designed. If you look at a Ford Expedition next to a Ford F-150, do you think Ford completely re-engineered the Expedition? No, it's obvious that Ford used the F-150 platform and modified it into the Expedition.

Ninety-seven percent of the parts are shared, three percent are different. Ninety-seven percent of the genes of an ape are shared with man, three percent are different. Yet, there isn't an evolutionist alive today that would suggest that the F-150 evolved by itself into Expedition, but that very same evolutionist will have you believe that an infinitely more complex machine, man, evolved from an ape despite all the evidence to the contrary. The more and more I study this, the more and more ludicrous their arguments become.

It has become obvious to me that the only reason the current powers-that-be are dismissing intelligent Design within the scientific community is that it implies a creator. This is the same reason that the Big Bang Theory took almost forty years to gain acceptance because it implied a creator. But finally, the weight of scientific evidence was so overwhelming that it overcame the bigotry and dogma of naturalism.

As for the Theory of Evolution, its proponents are feeling the heat which is becoming obvious by their increasing hysteria, as evidenced by Richard Dawkins, a professor of biology at Oxford, who said, "It is absolutely safe to say that if you meet somebody who claims not to believe in evolution, that person is either ignorant, stupid or insane (or wicked, but I'd rather not consider that)." Now let's take a look at this comment. First, it is unbelievably arrogant as there are scientists of equal or greater intellectual status than Richard Dawkins who are not Christians that dispute evolution. Additionally, Dawkins himself admitted that there is a chance that there is a God, however slight, yet refuses to look at evidence on both sides of this issue. Ironically, because of this attitude, he has become a "fundamentalist" for atheism ignoring and demonizing any one or theory that doesn't fit his naturalistic dogma. An additional irony is found in his book, *Climbing Mount Improbable* where he inadvertently proves intelligent design when he explains how scientists have recently "created" a program that shows how DNA can "randomly" make new body parts. It took intelligence to make this program, so if there is such a "program" in DNA, it had to be created.

But more importantly, Dawkins' quote is completely disingenuous and uses a typical tactic taken by evolutionists. When he says if you don't believe in evolution you're ignorant or stupid, he is using microevolution as proof for all of evolution, which is the same mistake that Darwin made, although in Darwin's case it was probably unintentional. As I said earlier, microevolution is a fact, but it is also what you would expect from a Creator who, as it's now becoming obvious from probability studies, created the universe with our galaxy in mind. And our galaxy was created with the earth in mind. And the earth was created with lesser life in mind as infrastructure for higher beings, with His ultimate creation being humans. So, it is obvious, or should be, that the creatures designed to inhabit the earth would be able to adapt and change to the changing environments of earth, which were created for them. It's all part of God's design. Now that last part is my opinion based on the evidence and is certainly not a strictly scientific view, but it is implied by the science.

Dawkins, as well as all leading evolutionists, know very well the problems with macroevolution but obfuscate them, because, as I alluded to earlier, the real reason that the theory of evolution is given a pass from a scientific perspective is because it is the lynchpin of their belief system. If you don't believe me, here is what Richard Lewontin, a well-known evolutionary biologist, has to say:

We take the side of science in spite of the patent absurdity of some of its constructs, in spite of its failure to fulfill many of its extravagant promises of health and life, and in spite of the tolerance of the scientific community for unsubstantiated just-so-stories, because we have a prior commitment, a commitment to materialism. It is not that the methods and institutions of science somehow compel us to accept a material explanation of the phenomenal world, but, on the contrary, that we are forced by our priori adherence to material causes to create an apparatus of investigation and a set of concepts that produce material explanations, no matter how counterintuitive, no matter how mystifying to the uninitiated. Moreover, that materialism is an absolute, for we cannot allow a Divine Foot in the door.

He says it well; because the Divine cannot be tolerated, materialists (naturalists) must be bigoted!

Now, here is a quote from a non-Christian. This quote is taken from *Darwin's Black Box*, by Michael Behe, Professor of microbiology at Lehigh. In his book he says the following:

Lynn Margulis, Distinguished Professor of Biology at the University of Massachusetts... says "that history will ultimately judge neo-Darwinism as a minor 20th century religious sect... " At one of her many talks she asks molecular biologists in the audience to name a single, unambiguous example of the formation of a new species by accumulation of mutations. Her challenge goes unmet.

Just in case this is not enough for you, there is a list of 700 (and growing) Ph.D. level scientists who are part of the "Dissent from Darwin" who have signed a statement that reads:

"We are skeptical of claims for the ability of random mutation and natural selection to account for the complexity of life. Careful examination of the evidence for Darwinian theory should be encouraged."

These scientists hale from the likes of Oxford, Yale, Princeton, Stanford, MIT, UC Berkley, UCLA and others. And many are leaders in their fields.

Isn't it ironic that Kansas is viewed by the national press and the establishment scientific community, as an educational backwater because the State School Board wanted to simply "allow an examination" of the Theory of Evolution. The truth is that Kansas is on the cutting edge of education. Years from now, Darwinism will be taught in the history books. Yet these modern day "flat earthers" are indoctrinating our children into the religion of materialism.

And that, my friends, leads me to Theistic Evolution.

Theistic Evolution is and always has been a complete cop-out. From the very start it was a way of conforming to the intellectual world. It started in the late 1800's and the early 1900's when theologians in the great Christian universities first in Europe and then in America, succumbed to their naturalistic intellectual peers and uncritically accepted evolution but said that God did it.

As its critics point out, it is an oxymoron; something cannot be random if guided by God. Yet today, most will say that initial creative act was done by God, but, despite the evidence against macroevolution, that we evolved by chance but at a point when we "were ready" God infused us with a soul and that we continue to evolve today. Now most lay people and theologians have not studied the evidence for evolution, nor have they thought through the implications of aligning themselves with what I consider the biggest false teaching that has ever been perpetrated on mankind.

From the start, the sole purpose of evolution was to lead people away from God. During Darwin's time, the Age of Enlightenment, the western world was coming out of a repressive time in the church, and naturalists were looking for an explanation of life apart from God so as to free themselves from the Church and usher in a new age of science. This was about the time that science was redefined to accepting only naturalistic explanations. Prior to this, it did not have this arbitrary, philosophical limitation.

Now, the implications of this are very profound. If there is no God then there is no absolute moral authority and no objective truth. Some of you will recognize this as the precursor of Post-Modern thinking. But the implications are much larger. Most of the evils perpetrated on the world, since the time of Darwin's Theory, have their roots or are enabled or perpetuated by the theory of evolution. In Hitler's book, *Mein Kampf*, he lays the groundwork for genocide when he says:

> "If nature does not wish that weaker individuals should mate with the inferior one; because in such cases all her efforts, throughout hundreds of thousands of years, to establish an evolutionary higher stage of being, may thus be rendered futile."

Hitler explains it very well, that the logical outgrowth of evolution is racism and genocide.

In case you think Hitler was a lone case, the modern day abortion movement was started by Margaret Sanger, a staunch evolutionist who wrote concerning the immigrants and the poor as; 'human weeds', 'reckless breeders', 'spawning human beings who never should have been born'. And she said this about blacks; "We do not want the word to go out that we want to exterminate the Negro population, if it ever occurs to their more rebellious members." She, along with Hitler, was a proponent and leader in the eugenics movement in which she exhorted Americans to "restrict the propagation of those physically, mentally and *socially inadequate*" in order to breed a better class of humans.

Oh, by the way, she was also the founder of Planned Parenthood.

In case you think these two are aberrations, let me ask you what is the greatest cause of human suffering and death in the world aside from nature? Now don't answer that, let me. The secular world will tell you it's religion. As our friend Richard Dawkins said, "I think a case can be made that faith is one of the world's great evils, comparable to the smallpox virus but harder to eradicate." People like Dawkins will always trot out the Crusades and the Inquisition in trying show the evils of religion but fail to recognize that secular regimes have murdered more people in the twentieth century than all "so-called" religious atrocities in the last 6,000 years combined. They are a drop in the bucket compared to Pol Pot alone who killed 2 million of his citizens in the killing fields of Cambodia. But it doesn't stop there; Stalin killed 30 million, and Mao 65 million of his fellow Chinese! And what do they have in common? All were leaders of secular regimes and atheist. This doesn't even include Hitler, who, as an atheist masquerading as a Christian, killed 6 million Jews. All of them used the Theory of Evolution to rationalize their secularism or atheism.

At this point I would like to ask your forgiveness. As an atheist for the first forty years of my life, I would like to apologize to you for being a part of this. I hope you will accept my apology.

So, now I ask myself, why in the world would Christians align themselves with evolution?!

Well, as I mentioned earlier, most (like I used to be) haven't objectively studied the evidence and the implications of evolution. And this is the vast majority of mainline Christianity. Over the years, I have had two well-meaning Christian friends tell me that I needed to read Francis Collins. You may know him as the scientist who led the Human Genome Project. He is also one of the leading proponents of theistic evolution. Their subtle suggestion was their way of letting me know that I was embarrassing myself with all this Intelligent Design "stuff". So, in an effort not to embarrass myself, I read *The Language of God*. I will say that the science, as it related to genomics (his specialty) was very interesting, but when he delves into areas that are not his specialty, that's where the book breaks down. As an example, he states, "it now seems likely that many examples of irreducible complexity are not irreducible at all, and that the primary scientific argument for ID is thus in the process of crumbling." If you read any of the comments on the so-called refutation of ID (and irreducible complexity in particular) you will find that this is naturalistic wishful thinking. There are other examples but let's just say he has a blind eye to the motivations of his materialistic colleagues.[2] So, what is his motivation to blindly follow evolution? That I can't answer but one thing is certain, theistic evolution is the only acceptable belief system that allows a scientist to maintain his or her respect of their naturalist colleagues, to get funding, and to gain tenure. Any other stance by a believer is a death knell to their career—the examples are many.

Secondly, some have and still will align themselves with evolution because it fits their religious worldview. As I said earlier, if macroevolution is true, then man must be evolving and therefore, religion must evolve to better serve a changing mankind. There is a group of so-called theologians known as the Jesus Seminar. These are ultraliberal theologians who deny the miracles and the resurrection of Jesus and are all theistic evolutionists. In what sense they are Christians, I can't fully grasp, but these are the folks you'll always see trotted out on national TV, the likes John Dominic Crossan and my favorite, Bishop John Shelby Spong, a former zoology professor and now an Episcopalian bishop who wrote the book, *Why Christianity Must Change or Die*. Does anyone see the irony in this? The once great Episcopalian denomination is now on the brink of extinction because of the very policies proposed by Bishop Spong. For this group, evolution allows them the freedom to reshape God, the Bible, and Jesus in their image and not like their "less educated" brethren who believe they were created in the image of God.

There is one last group that can fall into both camps above. Some Christians align themselves with evolution in order to distance themselves from their more fundamental brothers and sisters who believe in Creation Science. Essentially, they are embarrassed by this group and see them as their crazy uncle that they would prefer to lock in the attic than have to deal with them. As for me, while I might not agree with Creation Science,

---

2 Note: When I first became a Christian, I didn't want to read anything that contradicted what had led to my conversion. But over time, I realized this was not workable as I continually heard in the mainstream press that some of the issues that had led me to be open-minded about creation had been refuted. So, I began reading the refutations. What I found out was that the secular press would only print the refutations and seldom printed the responses. After reading the naturalistic critics and then the responses by the Socratic scientists, not a single ID principle has been refuted, this includes Irreducible Complexity contrary to what Collins claims in his book.

I nonetheless would never question their commitment to God, Jesus, and the truth of the Gospels. And to align yourself with false teaching just to feel good about your intellect just isn't right. Didn't Jesus say, *"If you're embarrassed of Me, I'll be embarrassed of you?"* And wasn't it God who said through the profit Isaiah, *"Woe to those who call evil, good, and good, evil!"*

Okay, let's wrap this up.

Here's why this debate is so important. First, since the advent of evolution and theistic evolution, the church has steadily declined to the point where it is almost non-existent in Europe, the birthplace of evolution and theistic evolution. The reason for this is that evolution is taught as a more rational explanation for life than God; that you don't have to have faith in anything but nature, which is around you all day. Theistic evolution, while an attempt to co-op evolution and the intellectual debate, only fosters doubt and doesn't alleviate it. Here again, evolution appears to be a more rational explanation and theistic evolution as a gimmick designed to dupe the unsuspecting.

Secondly, your children are being indoctrinated into a secular worldview under the guise of intellectual integrity. The Theory of Evolution is being taught as a fact, a fact that is not lost on your kids. Your kids know the implications. That's why I turned from God and most of the people I know turned from God because religion was irrelevant to them because it was viewed as a myth and a crutch for the weak.

Lastly, most of the people who don't believe in God don't believe in creation. It is the single most important aspect of faith, more important than the Bible and more important than Jesus. If someone doesn't believe in creation, it is impossible to believe in the saving grace of Jesus! *"In the beginning God created the heavens and earth!"*

Let me give you another example of this other than myself. Antony Flew was one of the preeminent atheist of the last half of the twentieth century. He had written more books on atheism than almost any other writer on the topic. But in 2004, he made an announcement that stunned the atheist community. He announced that he concluded that some sort of intelligence must have created the universe. In talking about biologists' investigation of DNA, he said this investigation *"has shown, by the almost unbelievable complexity of the arrangements which are needed to produce [life], that intelligence must have been involved. Has science discovered God?"* Now, he has since passed and we'll probably never know if he became a Christian, but he had started his faith journey because of science, not in spite of it. This illustrates the importance of this issue in terms of evangelism and leading people to the truth of Creation, God, and ultimately the saving grace of Christ Jesus.

Now you can do with this teaching as you see fit. I'm not going to tell you that you have to go out and read books and study. But you have to decide for yourself if this is as important as I think it is. For those of you who think I'm full of it, I encourage you to prove me wrong—please, please, please! Because I know, if you have an open mind, where it will lead.

Let me finish with a quote from the Apostle Paul that explains that this is not a new issue but one that must be constantly confronted and explains why the world is the way it is. In Romans 1:25 he says, *"They exchanged the Truth of God for a lie and worshiped and served created things rather than the Creator...Amen".*

Suggested Readings

A Case for Creation, by Lee Strobel

Darwin's Black Box and *A Mousetrap for Darwin*, by Michael Behe

Darwin's Doubt, by Stephen C. Meyer

After reading these books, read the following and ask yourself which has the stronger argument and looks honestly at both sides of the argument.

The God Delusion, by Richard Dawkins

The Language of God, by Francis Collins

The Love Dolt

(Think of the song for the "Love Boat")

This chapter on love is tough for most "real" men. I asked Brian to lock the doors once I started so that none of the men can get up and run out. The reason I say that is because, in my former life, talking about love was comparable to talking about oral surgery and I think that I'd rather have a dental procedure than talk about love!

I attribute this amoraphobia (you like that? I just coined it) to several factors. First, I'm a guy—what can I say. Secondly, my rural Midwest upbringing. Growing up in a farming community in Iowa, people just didn't talk about love. Even girls didn't talk about it in mixed company. But if you were a guy, it just wasn't done—it was taboo—unless you wanted to get beat-up, or worse yet, get called names (you fill in the blank). Men in Iowa lived by the creed that you don't have to tell someone you love them; they should just know it. The only time it was acceptable to utter the "I love you" words was if there was something to be gained, like...well, use your imagination. Here, I'll help you; like the Bud Lite commercial where the guy says to his dad, "I love ya, man!" so he could get the last beer. (Now, that's what you were thinking, wasn't it?)

Okay, let's get to the last reason and the primary reason. I was ignorant of what love truly was. I was a love dolt! I don't think I fully understood it until I became a Christian and that is really what this chapter is about. What is love or better yet, what is true, biblical love? Now I don't have all the answers to that question, but I certainly have a far better understanding than I did.

Before, if someone asked what love was, I would answer like nine out of ten guys would; you'd know it when you see it or better yet, when you felt it. You see, for me, and most of the western world, love is this nebulous thing that is hard to define. It's an emotional feeling that comes over you. A feeling of euphoria or a feeling of despair or a feeling of deep longing, depending on the situation, but a feeling nonetheless. So, you can see why I always had trouble with the biblical concept of love your neighbor. So, here's how it worked; you can't love someone unless you're in love (or have feelings for them) so when the Bible says to love your neighbor, how is that possible? How can you have feelings for someone you don't know or don't like? It was a conundrum for me. It seemed to me that this Bible stuff was just not possible so how could I possibly just believe? That's why it took facts and evidence for me to first believe and why I encourage you to study the evidence for God and the Bible, and to put things in their proper context, because that definition of love I just gave is not the biblical definition of love but a more modern or western definition, which is commonly referred to as "romantic" love.

But what is biblical love?

As you may know, the Bible was written in three different languages: Hebrew, Aramaic, and Greek. The word for love was not used in the Aramaic text, so we'll look at just the Hebrew and Greek words for love. In Hebrew, there is one primary word for love, "ahava". Now, before I go any further with that, I think it would be helpful to compare and contrast Hebrew and Greek. In the Semitic Hebrew language, there are no words for abstract thought. Whereas in Greek, and western languages, there are, which is why there are approximately 5 million words in Greek and 45,000 in Hebrew. For example, let's look at Psalm 103:8, *"the Lord is compassionate and gracious and slow to anger…"* Now, compassionate, gracious and anger are all abstract thoughts, so we know that the original Hebrew was translated into these abstract words. Let's look at "anger." The Hebrew is "awph" which is nose or more precisely "the flaring of your nose." So, what do you do when you get angry? You guessed it; you flare your nose. So, in Hebrew, if you wanted to express an abstract thought you had to use an analogy like in the example I just gave, and everything depended on the context. That's why in Hebrew, subtleties in their story telling were very important and most of these subtleties were and are lost on the western (Greek) minds because we have words to convey these thoughts. That's also one of the reasons that Jesus spoke in parables. In the Jewish culture, stories were an important part of conveying ideas and are much more memorable.

So, let's get back to "ahava." The root word for Ahava is "give", and it is modified by the letter "aleph" and changed from give to "I give" or also "love." So, love is a verb, a verb of action. It's something you do, not feel. By giving of yourself to another person, whatever form that giving takes; physical, emotional, intellectual—you are creating a connection, and only by continuing to give do you create a lasting connection.

Now the Greek language is a whole 'nother story. In the Greek language, the language of the New Testament, there are four words for "love" yet only two are used in the New Testament: agape and phileo. Phileo is commonly referred to as brotherly love, not family love but more like kinsmen love, while agape is the highest form of love. Some call it divine love, but it is also unconditional love for others despite their human frailties. This is by far the most commonly used word for love in the New Testament. It's interesting that the other two words, storge (love between a parent and a child) and eros (romantic/sexual love) are not found in the Bible, and these two words are most commonly associated with the English word "love".

Let's look at our modern usage of the word love. Let's take Romeo and Juliet for an example. They are idealized as poster children for romantic love. But…did they love each other, or did they covet what they knew they couldn't have? And think about it—it didn't turn out real well, did it? What did they "give" each other? Let's see, what did they give…a sentimental poem and brief romantic interlude. They didn't even give their lives for one another—they took their own lives out of despair—how tragic! The real tragedy is that this little story is used as a great example of "true love". Haven't you ever wondered what would have happened if they hadn't died? Maybe they would have lived happily ever after but more than likely they would have gotten bored with one another after the thrill of "love at first sight" had passed and moved on to a new thrill because they hadn't laid the foundation for true love. I don't know, maybe I'm just an old cynic? (I like to think that I've been blessed with the gift of cynicism.)

But this does beg the question; is emotion, or feelings, love? I think biblically the answer is a resounding "No!" Now, don't get me wrong, emotions can be a wonderful thing. The feeling you get when you meet someone you think you love. The feeling of longing…all the emotions, good and bad, that happen around love are great, but they are the result of love, not love itself. Is it any wonder that in America and most western cultures that the divorce rate is out of sight? It's because we think love is an emotion. "I just don't love her anymore". "I don't have any feelings for him". "The love is gone". All these clichés that people use to falsely describe love or the lack of love in a relationship.

But what does the Bible say about love? The quintessential passage on love is in 1 Corinthians 13: *"Love is patient, love is kind. It does not envy, it does not boast, it is not proud. It is not rude, it is not self-seeking, it is not easily angered, it keeps no record of wrongs. Love does not delight in evil but rejoices with the truth. It always protects, always trusts, always hopes, always perseveres. Love never fails…"*

What's missing from that passage? That's right, it says nothing about emotion. I don't see anything there that says, "love is tingly, love is sweaty palms, or love is an emotional high."

Breann (the worship leader) nailed it when she emailed me asking what the topic was for my talk. I was in a hurry, so I replied, "biblical love". This was totally unsatisfying to her, so she wrote back and ask, "Can you give me a bone? Is it love relating to husband/wife, friend, neighbors, God loving us...it's a pretty broadly defined word in the English language." My initial smart-alecky response when I read the email was, "Yes". But as I explained to her, biblical love makes no differentiation. The passage above in 1 Corinthians is used for weddings but the context of the passage is not about marriage, its simply about "love" and what love is!

I remember when I first read *A Case for Faith*; there was a chapter in which the author interviewed a theologian named Lynn Anderson. This guy I could really relate to as he had struggled much of his life with doubt. There always seem to be an aspect about Christianity that troubled him, and he was constantly asking why and working through these doubts. In the book, he relayed a story in particular that really stuck out to me and initially started me thinking about true love. In this story, he was counseling a husband who said he didn't "love" his wife anymore. Anderson's response was, "go home and love your wife". And the husband's response was, "but I don't have feelings for her anymore". Anderson's response was, "I wasn't talking about how you feel, go home and love her". The husband came back with, "But it would be emotionally dishonest to treat her that way when I don't feel it". So, Anderson asked, "Does your mother love you?" He said, "Of course she does". Then Anderson went on, "About three weeks after your mother took you home from the hospital and you were screaming with dirty diapers and she had to get up dog tired and put her feet on cold floor, clean up your miserable diapers, and feed you—do you think she got a bang out of it?" He answered, "No". Anderson responded by saying, "Well, then, I think your mother was being emotionally dishonest".

The point he was making was that love, like faith, is not about emotion. That like faith, people have the misconception that love is about feelings. That peoples' love ebbs and flows based on their feelings. That once their emotional high has faded, just like faith, so does their love. As Anderson said, "Faith, (like love), is not always having a positive emotional outlook toward God and life." I like what a friend of mine says, "If you have faith in God, you need to be prepared for disappointment". The same thing is true for love. As all married people know, you will be disappointed and be a disappointment, but true love endures all these ups and downs.

Paul stated this same concept in Romans 13 when he said, "*...whatever other commandments there may be, are summed up in this one rule: Love your neighbors as yourself. Love does no harm to its neighbor. Therefore, love is the fulfillment of the law.*" As always, Jesus said all that really needed to be said about love. What did Jesus say as they greatest commandment? "*To love the Lord God with your heart, soul and mind, and to love your neighbor as yourself.*" Now, He also said in the Sermon on the Mount, "*So in everything, do to others what you would have them do to you, for this sums up the Law and the Prophets.*" So, Paul and Jesus are saying that the "Golden Rule" is what love is. Jesus has cut through all the confusion for us westerners and made it very simple for us. Even I can get that. From this, I hope you can see where I arrived at the conclusion that love is not an emotion; emotion is the result of love.

Let me tell you a little story that I think illustrates the concept of biblical love. In 2007 we had a family reunion at the lake. It was an unusual event, to say the least. Kathy's Aunt Dee, who died of cancer about seven years before, had a child out of wedlock back in 1957. Those were the days when young women went away to have their babies. None of her brothers even knew she was pregnant, and they didn't even know this baby existed. Before Dee died, she told her daughter, Teri, about the baby and how she had gone to Washington State, had the baby, and had given him up for adoption. About a year and a half before the reunion, Teri received a call from an investigator from Washington State. Teri asked the lady, "You're calling about my brother, aren't you?" The lady was surprised and asked her if she would like to meet James. So, for the next year they talked and met, and decided that the families needed to meet, which was the family reunion at the lake.

Aunt Dee's family came; the aunts and uncles came with their families; Teri and her brother came and brought their families. James brought his adoptive mother and adoptive sisters along with their families.

It was interesting for me, since I'm not a blood relative; I was able to just hang back and watch it all unfold. Everyone was instantly accepted and made to feel as though there wasn't this fifty-year divide. Sure, there was some apprehension at first, but that soon faded. Soon everyone was telling stories about their families and there were a lot of Dee stories—what a great lady she was!

James, at some point in his earlier life was a professional saxophone player. It was his anniversary, so when the whole group was together, he surprised his wife and played her a Kenny G love song. All the women teared-up (all the men were thinking, "Great, I guess a vacuum cleaner is out for an anniversary gift this year.") But then he dedicated a song to his adoptive mother, Vicky, and to Dee, his birth mother. He played Amazing Grace! There wasn't a dry eye in the house. I tear-up now thinking about it. But what an appropriate song. Not only did Dee do a very loving and grace filled thing by giving up her baby to someone who could better love and care for him at the time, but it was his adoptive Mother, Vicky, who encouraged James to seek out his birth family and not to give up when obstacles occurred.

When I was leaving (I had to leave early), Vicky came to me and gave me a hug and a kiss and said, "Thank you for the love you and your family have shown us!" The love your family has shown us! She obviously gets and lives biblical love. "Love is patient, love is kind. It does not envy, loves is not proud..." I can't think of a better example of biblical love.

So, whether it's your neighbor, your wife or a long lost relative, love is what you do and how you treat people, not how you feel at the moment and if you follow this, emotion will follow.

It looks like I've now come full circle. I'm back to what most Iowans know; you'll know love when you see it.

Now, there is one last question we need to ponder; how do we know God loves us? I really struggled with that. For most of my life I didn't recognize God's love. I didn't even believe there was a God. I actually thought when I heard people say "God loves you" that they were silly and slightly deluded. How could they possible know that? It wasn't until I realized that Creation was true, and that the Bible was true, that I realized that God does indeed love us. Creation by itself shows us His love. He gave us this world and everything in it. He gave us life. He designed a world where the sun rises every morning to sustain us. He gave us an earth that provides for all our needs. He gave us free will so that we are able to love each other and to love Him. But most importantly, as John said in his gospel, *"For God so loved the world that he gave his one and only Son, that whosoever believes in him shall not perish but have eternal life."*

Jesus' resurrection is all the proof we need to know that God loves us!

11th Commandment

You may remember when Bryan gave a sermon that mentioned Martin Luther and his act of defiance toward the Catholic Church when he nailed his "95 Theses" on the door of the Wittenberg church.

Vera Hendricks, who was in attendance that day, took this episode to heart. You may remember Vera and know that she was, and maybe still is, an atheist. Vera, the physicist with her strong German accent, and being the *quiet and demure* person that she is, she decided to re-work the Ten Commandments and nail them to the Morse Church door. Now I must say I didn't agree with what she had done to the first ten but I absolutely loved her addition of an 11th Commandment: "Thou Shall Think!"

Far too long, modern Christians have given up the intellectual high ground to the secular community and hidden behind spiritualism. But this is not the history of the Church. For Centuries most scientists were men of faith. Most western scientist, men like Isaac Newton, Galileo, Kepler, Copernicus, and Pasteur, just to name a few, were Christians and many attributed their desire to seek knowledge to God and his Creation. They saw the order in nature and wanted to discover the intricacy of God's Creation. Newton is quoted as saying, "The most beautiful system of the sun, planets, and comets, could only proceed from the counsel and dominion on an intelligent and powerful Being."

It wasn't until the 18th century came that this all began to change. Then, in the 1800s, we had the "perfect storm" of Existentialism, the Higher Critics, and Darwin along with other humanistic philosophies. Existentialism is a philosophy that gained popular status among some intellectuals of the time and is the precursor to today's Postmodernism. Existentialism states that "we are what we can become" and "Our view of the world is enough to become Truth, because it is based on our facts." The Higher Critics were biblical scholars who began to the question the veracity of the Bible and pointed out supposed errors from an archeological stand-point, including several supposed errors in Luke/Acts. (Just a little aside; archeology of the 20th century verified that Luke was correct and that the Higher Critics were wrong). And of course, we all know who Darwin was.

These new events in the intellectual marketplace brought forth the Age of Enlightenment where intellectuals were freed from, as they felt, dogmatic teachings of the church, and Christianity was now viewed as a myth as opposed to truth. And then in the early 1900s, the European and east coast seminaries (like Harvard, Yale and Princeton) accepted evolution (writ large) but said the God did it, and theistic evolution was born and the fate of intellectualism within the church, for the time being, was sealed.

But today, we as Christians should not accept the status quo opinion of secular society but we should follow the words of Jesus and *"worship in spirit and in truth!"* For this reason, it is time that we put on our thinking caps and THINK! (I liked her 11th Commandment so much that I made a 'thinking cap' that says, "11th Commandment".)

I truly believe we are living in a unique time as it relates to the evidence for God and his Creation. We are now able to peer into the inner reaches of the cell and the outer reaches of the universe and it screams creation and not randomness!

Okay, it's time to put on our thinking caps. Let's take the Big Bang. Atheists today try to use it against Creation. But the dirty little secret that ill-informed atheists don't know (or try to obfuscate), is that it took almost forty years for the Big Bang to gain acceptance because of its *religious implications!* You see, naturalists had always believed (not known) that the universe was eternal because there are only two options; either the universe is eternal or something outside the universe is eternal because you can't get something from nothing. And if the universe was eternal you had eternity for randomness to cause life. But the Big Bang implied that there was a beginning. And worse yet, it implied a "big banger" or, heaven forbid, a Creator because there had to be a cause—someone to light the fuse, so to speak. But finally, the evidence and the explanatory value of the Big Bang theory overcame atheistic dogma and bigotry, and it has now become, among scientists, universally agreed as the most plausible explanation for how the universe began. Lastly, it also harmonizes very well with the Genesis account of creation. In fact, the ancient Hebrews were the only religious peoples whose creation story had its cosmology correct.

Now let's look at something from a philosophical standpoint. If you've done any reading or had any discussions with people about religion, or if you're just listening to everyday conversation, you've undoubtedly heard someone say the following: "you shouldn't force your morality on other people." In this age of hyper-tolerance, this is a common cliché. Okay, it's time to put on our thinking caps. Your next question should be, "Why?" You'll probably get, "Because it's just not right!" Then your response should be, "Is that your moral view?" You see; their original statement is contradictory or self-defeating. They're telling us not to do what they are doing to us, forcing their morality on us. By saying "shouldn't" and "not right" they are making a moral statement. So, whose morality trumps whose? Is their morality superior to ours?

You've also probably heard the following: "All religions are equally true and valid." This is commonly referred to in theological terms as "plurality." Sounds very high minded, doesn't it? Well, let's put on our thinking caps and examine this. Let's see; Buddhists are pantheist and say all is god, Hindus are polytheistic and have millions of gods, Islam says there is one god and Mohammed is its prophet, Christianity says Jesus is the Messiah, and Judaism says the Messiah has not come yet. Lastly, atheist say there is no god—yes, atheism is a religion. So, who's right? Therein lies the problem; they can all be *wrong* but they all can't be right. Even though there are some similarities, they all make mutually exclusive claims, and cannot possibly all be correct. So, either one is right or they're all wrong. Those are the only two options. It's like a five-part math question, even if you get four of the five parts correct, your answer is still wrong.

Now let's look at another common remark; "You shouldn't try to change other people's religious views." Again, it sounds very high-minded and tolerant. So again, let's put on our thinking caps. Your next questions should be, "Then why are you trying to change my religious views?" Again, the original statement is contradictory or self-defeating. They are doing to you exactly what they are telling you not to do. They either don't know, or don't care, that the Bible says we are to go forth and make disciple of all nations. So, by telling us we shouldn't try to change people's religious views, they are trying to change our religious views.

Okay, let's look at a corollary argument. If you've heard the previous one, you've probably heard this one, "All paths lead to god". Okay, let's put on our thinking caps and think about this. "All paths lead to god"; this is one that you can actually agree with. Let me explain; the Bible says that we will all stand before God and be judged. So, in effect, all paths do lead to God but (here is your chance to evangelize) you need to ask them, "Do you want to go to God as your judge with the baseline being perfection or do you want to go to God as your father with the baseline being grace?" That's an easy one for me and those who are open-minded.

Most of the remarks and clichés like this that you hear people say that may sound intelligent, simply don't hold up under scrutiny. And most people who say them have never been challenged and don't know how to respond. Most Christians I know are afraid to confront this type of thinking because, 1) they don't recognize it, 2) they don't think their faith needs defending or 3) they don't feel equipped intellectually to respond. But let's face it, most people who say these kinds of things aren't Christians because *they don't believe it's true* and therefore, it's not relevant to them. And most half-hearted Christians are only half-convinced that it is true and it shows. So how are you going to reach those people; the friends, relatives, or neighbors who at best are hedging their bets in case it is true or at worse think religion is irrational. These folks think you believe that "1 plus 1 = 3"? How are you going to show them that what you believe is 1+1=2 and that what they believe is 1+1=3?

Well, I can tell from my experience, it's through truth. Or another name for it is apologetics. It is a myth that religion is all about faith. Sure, there is faith involved in Christianity, but the underlying foundation is truth. And the Judeo/Christian religion is the only religion based on verifiable historical facts. All other religions expect you to blindly follow the teachings of their sages or prophets. That's called an "irrational belief". And if the Creation and the Resurrection are not true, your faith would also be irrational, and therefore, useless. Paul summed it up very well when he said in 1 Corinthians 15:13-14, "*If there is no resurrection of the dead, then not even Christ has been raised. And if Christ has not been raised, our preaching is useless and so is your faith.*"

Now in case you think this truth stuff is just me speaking, let's look at 1 Peter 3:15. "*...Always be prepared to give an answer to everyone who asks you to give the reason for the hope that you have. But do this with gentleness and respect...*"

Let's take a look at this passage in its cultural and historical context. Peter was an eyewitness to the crucifixion and resurrection of Jesus. Do you think he went up to people and said, "You just need to believe!" (as a well-meaning Christian once told me). No, of course not. He filled them in on what he saw and how the scriptures were fulfilled.

Now, let's look at the people who he was addressing. Based on his location in "Babylon" which most scholars suggest as code for Rome, he is writing to Jewish and gentile Roman believers. Peter and his fellow

Christians had to convince a very skeptical audience that the resurrection was true. Can you imagine an observant Jew believing in the messiah just because some Gentile believer said he had warm fuzzies about a man name Jesus! No. Or could you image a Roman citizen "just believing" in Jesus because a Christian told him he should, believing in someone who was an enemy of Caesar and whose association with that person could get them thrown in jail or in with the lions or your body used as a streetlight. He or she had to "be prepared" by providing the reasons for their hope in Jesus or they had to be prepared to send them or lead to someone or something that could help them with their skepticism. And let's take Paul. He went to the desert for two years with his scrolls to prove to himself that Jesus was who He said he was. And what did he do when he first hit town on his evangelizing missions? He would *reason* with the Jews in the synagogue, and then he would reason with the local gentiles as he did with the Greeks at Mars Hill.

You see, modern Christianity has become a "feel good" religion where people are told they just need to believe because of some esoteric truth that they'll understand once they believe. Well, I'm sorry but that is mysticism or, at worst, Gnosticism, something the early church recognized and banished from the church 1900 years ago. Unfortunately, it has reared its ugly head again, as it does periodically.

Also, mainstream Christianity has become "hands off" as it relates to evangelism. If you act "Christianly" enough, people will be drawn towards you and by your actions, you will lead them to Christ. You don't want to tell people about Jesus because you might offend them. Well, as Jesus said, and Paul reiterated, the gospel is offensive to non-believers, so we need to get over ourselves and quit worrying about offending people (that's personally a hard one for me). Now I'm not saying you need to get a flashing neon cross and carry it up and down Main Street telling people they need to repent (I actually saw this in New Orleans). What I'm saying is that just because there is a possibility that you might offend someone if you bring up religion, that shouldn't keep you from bringing it up.

Now I know that both of these systems of conversion do work on occasion, that people do have spiritual awakenings, and that we as Christians must live lives that are pleasing to God and thereby will draw some people to the Church, and that to gain creditability with people, most often you need to have some sort of relationship with them. BUT, biblically and practically, they are insufficient to reach most non-believers. Only when these methods are combined with Truth will we truly be able to reach the lost among us. Here again, this is not me speaking. All you have to do is look at Jesus' own words when He said, *"Believe me when I say, I am in the Father and the Father is in me, or at least believe on the **evidence** of the miracles themselves."* (emphasis added) Now, did Jesus ask people to "just believe?" Yep. And did they "just believe?" Nope. Some did but most didn't. It wasn't until he *proved* who He said he was with miracles and His resurrection that people actually believed, and they believed in droves! All throughout history, the Church flourishes when truth and spiritualism mesh as in Acts or the reformation or the great awakenings.

I can tell you unequivocally, that I would not be a Christian today if it weren't for the Truth of Creation, The Truth of the Bible, and the Truth of the Resurrection. It just wouldn't have happened unless Jesus himself had appeared to me. Even after I knew that it was true, I still didn't act on it for about a year because I wasn't real sure I wanted to be identified as a "true believer" and all the implications that brings with it. It wasn't until I was around Christians for a while, that I realized that some were actually normal and not wild eyed, mind-numbed zealots. So, relationships do matter, but only up to a point, then Truth with the nudging of the Holy Spirit must take over.

You know, now that I think about it, Jesus did appear to me. He appeared to me in the words of the Bible, once I knew they were true!

I'm going to fill you in on a little secret; in my five years as a Christian, I have come to realize that I am unique within the church, somewhere on the level of Dave (our resident Jew) and Vera. I've also found that most lifelong Christians don't get where I'm coming from. But that's all right because, outside the Church, I am (or was) the norm. People aren't staying away from the Church because the Pastors gave a bad sermon or because "churches just want your money", or because "the church causes evil in the world". No, they don't come because it's not relevant to them because they don't believe it's true. In most churches, only about twenty percent or so regularly attend church. And if Bryan's demographic studies are correct, that means that only ten percent are committed Christians. The rest are either hedging their bet in case it's true or they are pacifying a spouse or family members.

So, what do we do about that?

I know for me, I feel like the church let me down. It could have taught me the things that I had to learn on my own, but they didn't because of some of the reasons I mentioned earlier. I've answered some of the following questions today but if you truly want to lead others to the Truth of God, you need to be reasonably conversant with the following questions:

> *Is there really a God?*
>
> *Why do you believe in miracles?*
>
> *Isn't Christianity just a psychological crutch?*
>
> *Is the Bible reliable?*
>
> *Why do the innocent suffer (why does God allow evil)?*
>
> *Is Christ the only way to God?*
>
> *Will God judge those who have never heard about Christ?*
>
> *Why are so many Christians hypocrites?*
>
> *Will my good works get me to heaven?*
>
> *Isn't salvation by faith too easy?*
>
> *What does the Bible mean by "believe"?*
>
> *Can anyone be sure of their salvation?*

There are so many resources to help you with this. Below are just a few of the books and authors that I have found helpful, both from an evidential and from a philosophical standpoint. These books are very easy reads and are more of a starting point that will lead you to many other resources. Have at it!

A Case for Faith by Lee Strobel*

A Case for Miracles by Lee Strobel

The Reason of God by Timothy Keller**

I Don't Have Enough Faith to be an Atheist by Norman L. Geisler and Frank Turek

*Strobel has written several "Case For" books. A Case for Faith covers multiple topics but only minimally touches on miracles which is why I included his latest book, A Case for Miracles.

** Tim Keller has several other very good books including Making Sense of God, and my favorite, Hidden Christmas.

Forgiveness

Most of you who have heard me talk know by now that I like to look at things from a little different perspective, that I tend to look at things from an intellectual basis as opposed to a spiritual basis and that I'm going to give you a perspective that you probably haven't heard before. Now, this is not to say that I'm some kind of intellectual, it's just that I'm more comfortable looking at things from this prospective. Besides, it was the way I came to Christ.

To reiterate, I'm not an intellectual. If intellect were compared to a bike race, an intellectual would be Lance Armstrong. As for me, you'd need to picture Pee Wee Herman riding his classic red bike with big fenders, ringing his little bell. He might finish the race, but no one would mistake him for one of the favorites. (Hopefully, I haven't seared that image into your head and ruined you for life.)

To me, context is everything. I personally think that one of the worst things you can do when reading the Bible is to randomly pick out a verse and then somehow apply how it makes you feel to your life. You hear about people doing this a lot. But the Bible is very clear that we are to test our feelings against the Word of God so that we are not swayed by our feelings. God programmed us and is trying to make us aware that feelings are fleeting but his Word is based on unchanging truth. As John said in 1 John 4:1, "Dear friends, do not believe every spirit, but test the spirits to see whether they are from God, because many false prophets have gone out into the world."

In addition, in reading the New Testament we have to refer back to the Old Testament or Torah. When Jesus taught, his audience certainly knew the Old Testament implications of His teachings. That's why they would act so seemingly unreasonably to apparently innocuous teaching of His, because they knew the Old Testament implications.

So, what I'm going to teach on today is one of those examples where I feel the traditional teaching of the Church does not take into account the Old Testament and the Jewish cultural context. While much of traditional Christianity views what I'm about to say in a different light, there are several theological scholars who support what I have to say. More importantly, I feel the Bible taken in context, also agrees with what I have to say.

Okay, let's get going. Forgiveness. How would you characterize the traditional teaching of the church? How about "forgive and forget". Most would use Mathew 18:21-22 as justification for this, '*Then Peter came to*

Jesus and asked, "Lord, how many times shall I forgive someone who sins against me? Up to seven times?"

Jesus answered, "I tell you, not seven times, but seventy-seven times."

Now, that sounds like we should forgive and forget, right? Right, only if it is taken out of biblical and cultural context. First, all you have to do is look at the first part of this discourse on forgiveness and you'll see that Jesus says to confront the person who has sinned against you and *"if he listens to you (or agrees with you), you have won him over."* If he doesn't and others agree with you, you are to eventually treat him like a "pagan or tax collector". Now, that doesn't sound like "forgive and forget" to me.

As to the cultural context, who was Mathew's gospel directed towards; who did he write it for? Jews. So, therefore, we have to look at the Jewish customs at that time, not Greek or gentile customs. In Jewish society, of which Jesus was a part, forgiveness was only given to someone who asked for forgiveness; or in other words, someone who repented and acknowledged their sin and offered restitution. Restitution could be in the form of money or property or simply recognition of how the offense affected the person. Furthermore, it was the Jewish custom of the time to forgive someone only three times, so Jesus expanding on this custom implying unlimited forgiveness shocked his audience and gave them a glimpse of God's grace and forgiveness towards them. What's also interesting about this passage is that this grace appears to only apply to believers; "if your brother sins…" with the implication being your fellow Jew. But it is clear from other passages that Jesus was alluding to harmony among the church, something Paul expanded upon in his epistles.

Now let's look at a corresponding passage in Luke 17:3-4: *"…If your brother sins, rebuke him, and if he repents, forgive him. If he sins against you seven times in a day, and comes back to you and says, 'I repent,' forgive him".* Isn't it interesting that in Luke, the repent part is added but it is left out of Mathew's version? The reason for that is all about context. Luke was writing to gentiles who didn't know Jewish customs. Whereas Mathew was written to Jews who would certainly know their own customs. Therefore, in Mathew, the audience would have known the whole custom of forgiveness and, therefore, repentance was implied.

So, let's look into why this distinction is important.

Today in society and in a large portion of the church, we have what is technically called "therapeutic forgiveness". This type of forgiveness says that you are to forgive someone whether or not they ask for forgiveness, and you are only to confront them if you feel right in doing so. In other words, if it benefits you. The whole process is about making you feel better and your feelings. It's the epitome of self-actualization, the "me first" mentality that infects our society. Now within much of the church, it is looked upon as a badge of honor to forgive someone unilaterally, that you are showing "Christ-like" attributes if forgiveness is granted under all conditions, whether it is asked for or not; therefore, whether it is deserved or not.

But isn't this type of forgiveness all about you and not about your neighbor? Biblically, would you say that putting yourself first is looked upon as a worthy attribute? No, of course not. What is? What did Jesus say were the greatest commandments? Yes, to *"love the Lord God, with all your heart, soul and mind!"* And secondly, *"love your neighbor as yourself"*. Help me here…where does it say to put your feelings above your neighbor? Where did Jesus say how you feel matters at all? It seems to me that once you've accepted God's grace, that He wants you to feel for your neighbor and those less fortunate than you. I'm sorry but I've yet to find the passage in the Bible that says, "If it feels good, do it!" However, the Apostle Paul does say in Philippians, *"Do nothing out of selfish ambition or vain conceit, but in humility consider others better than yourselves. Each of you should look not only to your own interests, but also to the interest of others."* Jesus says to follow his commandments by loving God and loving your neighbor by serving them. But here's the really cool part; by doing these things you will feel good because your life will have meaning and purpose, and not just an endless pursuit of self-gratification. Let me tell you, this little rant strikes home to me as much as any of you listening to me.

So, what is the biblical formula for forgiveness? Well, let's go to God for the answer. How are we forgiven by God? What's the process? That's right, we ask for forgiveness (or repent) and God forgives us. Does God forgive us if we don't ask? Nope. It is a two-way street. Both parties must act.

There is a passage in Colossians (Col 3:13) where Paul says, *"forgive as the Lord forgave us."* I would love to use this passage to prove my point by saying, 'see we are supposed to forgive in the manner that God forgives us', but I'd be violating the rule of context. Because he really meant it in a different way when you read the whole passage. What he is really saying, we should forgive others because God forgave us. The full passage reads, *"Therefore, as God's chosen people, holy and dearly loved, clothe yourselves with compassion, kindness, humility, gentleness and patience. Bear with each other and forgive whatever grievances you may have against one another. Forgive as the Lord forgave you."* While this passage in context doesn't support or contradict my point, it is a wonderful passage on forgiveness and leads us toward the purpose of forgiveness.

So, what is the purpose of forgiveness? Well, why did Jesus come? To restore our relationship with God. Jesus provided our restitution. His death on the cross paid for our sins and provides our restitution and completed the act of forgiveness so that we could have fellowship with God through Jesus. So, forgiveness is about reconciliation and the restoration of relationships; it's about restoring your relationship with your "neighbor". It's not about making yourself feel good at the expense of your relationship with your neighbor.

So, what do we do if someone does something that separates us from one another? Biblically, if someone has truly wronged you, or sinned against you, you need to go to the person and let them know the situation. Here's why; God created us, he designed our human nature and He knows that most of as humans hold grudges no matter how "good" a Christian you are, no matter how hard you try, that most of us we will hold grudges. While some of us can continue to have some sort of relationship with that person that isn't adversarial or hostile, with most of us there is underlying discord. It's inevitable, it's who we are as humans. Unrepented sin goes against God's nature and since we were created in His image, it goes against our nature as well. If we put on a "good face" and pretend nothing is wrong, for most of us, it will either lead to guilt because we'll feel that if we were "good" Christians, we'd be able to forgive this person, or it will lead to resentment because of the injustice or resentment because we feel guilty even though we were wronged. And I can tell you that a lot of Christians feel guilt because they are unable to "forgive and forget" unilaterally.

I have a good friend whose father walked out on the family when she was in grade school. Her whole life she felt as though she was somehow inadequate because she was unable to forgive her father. Everyone told her she needed to just forgive him and forget about it, but she couldn't because he never showed any remorse. He would occasionally come around and act as if nothing happened. So here is a little girl, who is not only traumatized by a negligent father but also is made to feel guilty by well-meaning Christians giving unbiblical platitudes. I know from talking to her that once she realized God's biblical plan for forgiveness, it was a huge weight off her shoulders. She no longer needed to feel guilty and even lessened her resentment toward her father.

This also resonates with me personally. The very year I became a Christian, I had a conflict arise with my siblings. Now my brother and sisters are, in some respects, my best friends. I tried to forgive and forget. I did what people told me; I wrote a letter explaining what they'd done and how it made me feel. You know the advice, 'write a letter but don't send it so you can get it off your chest.' But it didn't work. I still felt resentment and I felt guilty—I just couldn't get over it. Here I was, a new Christian, and I was already flunking one of my first major tests because I thought I needed to forgive them by myself. Then one day, through a third party, they realized what they'd done, and they called me and apologized. It was one of the best days of my life. (Don't tell anyone but I actually cried it was such a relief.) How many times has someone told you they were sorry and all the anger and resentment you held toward that person just melts away? It's surprising how quickly it fades away. But it really shouldn't be surprising—it's how God designed us and what God planned for us.

So, what if you don't like conflict and don't want to confront the person? Let's think about that. Are you letting that person off the hook if you don't go to them? If they did something harmful to you on purpose, then they need to be confronted. And if it was unintentional, I don't know about you, but I'd like to be told if I'm doing something that has wronged someone. I certainly don't want to be a jerk and sometimes we need to be told when we're being one.

This leads to another question; What if the person you go to blows you off and doesn't acknowledge what they've done? Or what if the person is no longer around?

Your only option is to give it over to God and have faith and trust that God will deal with this situation in His time and His way. We trust that God will give us salvation through Jesus; we also have to trust God in other areas of our lives. Not only is God a God of love but He also is a God of justice.

Now some of you may be thinking that "giving it over to God" is a cop out. But what are your options? You can't shoot 'em *"Thou shall not murder"*; you can't plot revenge, *"Vengeance is mine, sayeth the Lord"*; you can't gossip to other people for as the proverb says *".... gossip separates the best of friends"* (16:28). So, your only option is to give it over to God and know that God will deal with it.

You may also see this "giving it over to God" as semantics; "aren't you just really forgiving that person?" No. Here is the controversial part; biblically, there is no forgiveness without repentance. As I said earlier, it is a two-way street. What you are really doing is trusting in God and showing grace; the same grace that Jesus showed to us.

Let's back up a little. Notice that I said, "If someone truly wrongs you or sins against you." Let's examine that a little bit. What would be someone sinning against you? Let's see, thou shall not murder, thou shall not steal, thou shall not commit adultery, thou shall not covet, thou shall not bear false witness, honor your father and mother…the rest have to do with God and not your neighbor. So, aside from the last one, honor your father and mother, (children!) how often do the other ones happen to you?

Now, obviously there are sins other than the Ten Commandments, but let's face it, we as humans sometimes look for reasons to be offended. How many times can you truly say that somebody, especially someone who is Christian, purposely tried to offend or harm you? Do you think people purposely go around thinking of ways to offend you? Think about yourself. When was the last time you purposely tried to offend or maliciously denigrate someone (aside from your spouse or siblings)? I know for me, the last time I can remember doing something like that was in ninth grade when I tried to pick a fight with a guy because he was bad-mouthing me. I couldn't bring myself to haul off and hit him, so I tried to pick a fight with him so I could beat the crap out of him. I called him names and made fun of him in front of a group of guys, but he wouldn't take the bait. And then I did it…I made fun of his nose, which was bigger than most at the time. Can you believe it; I made fun of his nose. But this thing (my nose) wasn't always like this. It didn't get like this until after "The Confrontation". *"Vengeance is mine, sayeth the lord."* It was not one of my proudest moments.

My point is (aside from the rare occasion) that most of the time we are offended it's usually unintended. And have we really been sinned against? I don't think so. I think much of the time we look for reasons to be offended or we attribute sinister motives to people who have no such intent. And most the time it's our pride that is the problem. We feel slighted for some reason. So, now who is the sinner and who is the 'sinnee'? As the proverb says, *"Pride only breeds quarrels…"*

But let's face it; there are a lot of EGR's (extra grace required) out there. And there are especially a lot of Christian EGR's. But we as Christians are to show grace to one another and accept people for how and who they are, since we are all creations of God.

Paul goes with this theme in Philippians 4:2-3 when he says, *"Now I appeal to Euodia and Syntyche. Please, because you belong to the Lord, settle your disagreement. And I ask you, my true partner, to help these two women, for they worked hard with me in telling others the Good News…"*

Here Paul is writing to the "perfect" church, and yet, this church that Paul cherishes because it is living out their faith, is having a squabble amongst two prominent members. It seems as though Paul is having a kum bah yah moment: "Can't we all just get along!" This is a consistent theme throughout much of his writings; we as Christians need to get along and not let petty, unbiblical differences get in the way. In other words, "show grace to one another!" And we're not even supposed to let petty biblical differences get in the way of church unity either. To paraphrase Paul, "in the essentials conformity, in the non-essentials liberty." I guess that message didn't get to all the denominations in time.

Just think if we did all get along, we could then concentrate our grace and forgiveness on those outside the church!

So, here's what we do; if you feel as though someone has wronged you in some way, examine the situation and see if it's not you that is the problem, and if not, go to the person. And if you feel like you did something wrong to someone, go to that person and ask forgiveness.

I've seen good relationships go bad because neither party would act. I think we all have. I've also seen good relationships grow because one of the parties had enough love for their "neighbor" that they confronted them, and the other person saw what they'd done and asked for forgiveness. That, my friends, is what forgiveness is all about.

Let me finish with the Apostle Paul who said in Colossians and Romans, *"Remember, the Lord forgave us, we must forgive others,"* and

"*Accept one another, just as Christ accepted you, in order to bring praise to God.*"

Amen.

Tithes and Offerings

I stand before you with the privilege of talking to you today about steward-ship. And a part of stewardship is money management. Isn't that cool? The guy who used to balance his checkbook by opening a new account every six months and closing the old account after I was sure all the checks cleared, gets to talk to you about money management. But that was a *long* time ago and I have seen the errors of my ways.

Much of this talk concerns tithing. Most people dread this talk and dread giving it. That's why I volunteered to speak on this subject, and really, I'm looking forward to it because I think it's a very important topic and one that I've come to appreciate. And I would bet that none of you have heard this version of the stewardship talk. For those of you who are guests, please know that we are not directing this talk to you but to our regular attendees. So, just sit back and enjoy and hopefully you'll find something of interest or something you haven't heard before.

Stewardship. Stewardship involves the managing of your time, tal-ents, and money given to us by God. Part of this involves the giving of your tithes or "first fruits" in the form of worship, spiritual growth, serving others and the church, and the giving of your money. I'm going to speak mostly on the last part because, well, Jesus spoke the most about that part.

In the Bible, Jesus talks about money more than any other topic except salvation. And I don't think that was a coincidence, as you'll hopefully see. Today, as in Jesus' time, money is an issue that dominates our lives; it either controls you or you control it. The passages that I think best exemplifies Jesus' teaching to the subject is Mathew 6:19-24:

"Do not accumulate for yourselves treasures on earth, where moth and rust destroy and where thieves break in and steal. But accumulate for yourselves treasures in heaven, where moth and rust do not destroy, and thieves do not break in and steal. For where your treasure is, there your heart will be also."

"The eye is the lamp of the body. If then your eye is healthy, your whole body will be full of light. But if your eye is diseased, your whole body will be full of darkness. If then the light in you is darkness, how great is the darkness!"

"No one can serve two masters, for either he will hate the one and love the other, or he will be devoted to the one and despise the other. You cannot serve God and money."

As you can see, this passage is broken up into three paragraphs. The first and the last paragraphs are fairly self-explanatory and essentially say the same thing, that money shouldn't be your treasure, that hording it does you no good in attaining your heavenly reward and can actually keep you from it. But the second paragraph is kind of odd and doesn't appear to fit with the others. In the first and last, He's talking about money and then right in the middle He starts talking about optometry. When you look at the commentary concerning this paragraph in the NIV Study Bible you get the following:

"Spiritual vision is our capacity to see clearly what God wants us to do and to see the world from his point of view. But this spiritual insight can be easily clouded. Self-serving desires, interests, and goals block that vision. Serving God is the best way to restore it. A "good" eye is one that is fixed on God."

Now, I don't doubt what this commentary is trying to say but it's not very satisfying as to why Jesus all the sudden changes his thought in mid-stream. When I first read the Bible, I thought this paragraph was very strange and out of place. But later, when Kathy and I started studying the Jewish roots of the Christian faith so we could put Jesus' teachings in their proper historic and cultural context, we discovered the answer to this apparent disconformity in Jesus' teaching. You see, a "good eye" was, and may still be, a Jewish idiom for being generous. Conversely, someone who has a "bad eye" is someone who is stingy. So, contrary to how it appears, Jesus is not changing His train of thought during this discourse on money but is being consistent. He is saying do not hoard your money because it will do you no good in heaven, but instead be generous with your money, and you will do good, set a good example for others, and you will be rewarded in Heaven. In biblical times saying something three times (as in "Holy, holy, holy") was the same thing as using three exclamation points at the end of a sentence. This topic was so important to Jesus that he said the same thing in three different ways so as to emphasize its importance.

Now, let's go to tithing. In the Old Testament, the tithe was one/tenth of your "first fruits" which was given to the priests for the support of the priesthood, temple, and the community. If you'll remember, the Levites (the priests) had no inheritance in the land. Therefore, they had to be supported by their communities and this was, in effect, a tax for the Hebrew theocracy. An offering, often called a freewill offering, was something given for a specific or general purpose over and above the tithe, out of your abundance.

Oddly enough, tithing is only referenced directly once in the New Testament when in Mathew and Luke, Jesus is chastising the Pharisees for giving their tithe but neglecting justice and the love of God. As with many things in the New Testament, tithing was assumed as it was a cultural norm for Jews to tithe. As for Jesus chastising the Pharisees, this is also a common theme throughout His teachings. The appearance of being pious is irrelevant; it's what is in your heart. So, here Jesus makes it clear that tithing in and of itself is not what is important, it's your motivation for tithing. However, under the Old Testament laws that were in affect at the time of Jesus' teachings, tithing was required of Jews. While it was required of the Jews, tithing was not required of the "God Fearers."

So, this begs the question; "are we as Christians required to tithe?" Before I answer that, I'm going to give you a short disclaimer; what I'm about to say is controversial—not all theologians agree with it. But what the heck...here goes.

Okay, let's go back to the God Fearers. These people were Gentiles that worshiped with Jews but were not of Jewish decent and had not converted through circumcision. God Fearers lived under the Noahic Laws. These laws were not part of the Torah (Old Testament) but inferred from Genesis Chapter 9 in the exhortations God gave to Noah and are part of the oral Mishnah (oral commentary of the Law) that was later codified in the Talmudic writings. According to Jewish tradition, the following rules or commandments are binding on all people, Jews and Gentiles alike. The original four Rules (which were later expanded to seven) are: No Idolatry! No Perversions! No strangled meats! No eating of blood! Now, some of you may recognize these rules as they are the same ones given to the gentile believers in Acts 15:28-29, *"It seemed good to the Holy Spirit and to us not to burden you with anything beyond the following requirements: You are to abstain from food sacrificed to idols, from blood, from the meat of strangled animals and from sexual immorality. You will do well to avoid these things. Farewell."*

So, you can see that non-Jews, before, during, and *after* the time of Jesus' were never required to tithe. So, clearly this indicates that we are not required to tithe. Additionally, we are saved by Grace alone. To require tithing would be putting the same yokes on us that Jesus chastised the Pharisees for.

Now that I've told you that tithing is not mandatory, I'm going to tell you why you should tithe!

While we are not required to tithe, we *are* asked to give. I think the verses that best sum this up are 2 Corinthians 9:6-7: *"Remember this: Whoever sows sparingly will also reap sparingly, and whoever sows generously will also reap generously. ⁷ Each of you should give what you have decided in your heart to give, not reluctantly or under compulsion, for God loves a cheerful giver."*

Now for a point of clarification, from here on out when I say "tithing" I'm referring to what we give or pledge to the church on a regular basis (which is really a free will offering). When I say "offering" I'm referring to everything given over and above your tithe, quite often one-time or temporary giving for a specific purpose or cause. So, if you gave to the "brick fund" or worked on the patio, this is an offering of your money or your time and is not part of your tithe. And your tithe should not be reduced by offerings out of "your abundance". Another way to look at is, tithes go to the church and the church directs where the money goes but with offerings you are directing where the money goes.

I remember before I was a Christian, Kathy used to drag me to church, and I remember the gyrations we'd go through to decide on how much we'd give. The way I figured it, the Church ladies were essentially baby-sitting my kids for an hour so ten bucks seemed fairly generous. I remember the dread when it came time to make a pledge and how the rationalizations always kicked in. Kathy would always lobby for giving the $10 per week ($20 bucks when we got a little older) even when we didn't go, and me, being the crypto-atheist, always had reasons why we couldn't afford it. I liked the "pay as you go" plan much better. It never occurred to me that we should give a percentage of what we earned primarily because I didn't see the relevance. I didn't see the need if we weren't their using the facilities and since I didn't believe, I couldn't really believe that anybody would actually give 10% to the church. I had always heard about "those" churches that browbeat their members to give 10% but we went to a church that never even requested a tithe of us. I remember, I once heard a rumor that one family in the church actually tithed and since the man of the family was an attorney, I had a good idea how much he was giving and I thought, if it were true, he must be a little touched and I wasn't real sure I'd call him if I needed an attorney.

But after coming to the realization that Creation, Jesus, and the Bible were true, and after I'd read the Bible, it was a no-brainer that we'd give 10% of our income to the church, not out of obligation but out of gratitude!

And you know what, we never even missed the money. We didn't consciously change our spending habits, it just worked out. Even today when our income has declined because of starting a new business, it's just a given that we're going to give our 10% and it just works out. Besides it's not our money anyway; it's just ours to use. Really, I can hardly wait to make more money so that I can not only give a larger tithe, but also give to organizations and causes that need assistance. I would love to be able to give more money to Grand Avenue Temple, for example, and KICK Ministry. One is doing God's work for the poor and the other is showing inner city kids how to live Christian lives through sports.

Now, part of what I just said use to really bug me. The part about it "not being our money". I used to think, the heck it's not my money…I worked hard for that money and nobody's going to tell me it's not mine! A lot of pastors throw that phrase around and just assume that people get it. But I certainly didn't get it and it use to anger me. It just seemed like a trite ploy to get people to cough up more money. But the more I thought about it, the more sense it made. Maybe I was just being obtuse, and this doesn't really bother anyone else, but here's how I came to reconcile that money is really God's. Okay follow me now; clearly the vast preponderance of evidence shows that the universe was created and that we are a part of that creation. And everything that we as humans create would not be possible without God and His initial creation. Therefore, it *is* all His. No different than when one of my minor children goes out and makes money; legally it's mine even though I allow them to use it for their benefit as long as it's done within the parameters that Kathy and I set. No difference. So, if God's wants his creations to give, I'm going to give. As with all things that we are asked to do in the Bible, it is for our benefit and not just arbitrary rules designed to oppress us.

Okay, I know that some of you are thinking, "How does tithing benefit me?" Glad you asked. First, by tithing we are being taught to be generous. It's a practical lesson in being generous and not hording. Now, the world teaches us the concept of scarcity. That we have to get and keep ours because if we don't someone else will take it. In other words, life is a zero-sum gain; if I make more it is at the expense of someone else who, therefore, makes less, so you'd be a fool to give up what you have for the benefit of someone else. But God teaches abundance, that there is plenty for everyone and the logical outgrowth of that is that if I give to someone else, there is plenty more where that came from. So, giving is a gift, a gift that not only benefits others but also benefits us by helping us to trust God more and to give up our dependence on money.

Secondly, and this one will probably seem a little self-serving, but clearly, we are rewarded for being generous. Again, this is a common theme "do good and you will be rewarded in Heaven" post salvation. Jesus makes this clear from Mathew 16:19 when He says, *"But accumulate for yourselves treasures in heaven."* Now, I've always struggled with this because it *does* feel self-serving; I'm giving money and doing good works because I'm going to get a bigger slice of the pie in heaven? It just doesn't feel right. To me, I do these things out of gratitude for God's creation and salvation. But, here again, the more I read and study this, the more I see the logic in it. Let's face it, we as humans are by nature self-serving in varying degrees. No matter how good a person we are, at times even the most unselfish of us, put ourselves ahead of others. Why not use that human trait for good by rewarding us for *doing* good? We reward are children for doing good, why wouldn't our heaven father reward us for doing good. If it takes a little heavenly motivation for us to experience the joy of giving, where's the harm in that?

Lastly, by giving to the church we are helping our neighbors as well as ourselves. There may come a time in your life that you'll find yourself in dire financial straits. I don't know of a single established church that doesn't have a fund to help its members if they find themselves in financial difficulty. Some of you think that this would never happen to you, but I have friends who were living the south Johnson County dream, only to find themselves struggling and then being financially supported by their church. That's what the tithe was meant for from the beginning; the support of the temple (church), the priests (the pastor) and the community (us).

Now, while all of these reasons are true, they are only tangential and pale in comparison to the most important reason of all for tithing your time, talents, and money. Let's look at Mathew 6:22-23 again but this time, let's substitute the literal meaning:

"How you handle money is the lamp of the body (*it indicates to the world you're standing in God's Kingdom*). If then *you are generous,* your whole body will be full of light (*the world will know by your actions that you put God first*). 6:23 But if *you are stingy,* your whole body will be full of darkness (*you set a bad, obvious example*). If then *your heart is obscured by your greed,* how great is the darkness (*your greed will keep you from knowing God*)!

So, it's clear from this passage and the other two passages that the giving of your money to God's Kingdom is a clear indication of where your heart is. If we, as a church did not ask you to give, we'd be doing you a disservice. Because, it is our responsibility, not only as a church but also as fellow Christians to help you grow in your faith!

Jesus says, *"Where your treasure is, there your heart will also be."* The way Billy Graham put it was, "Give me five minutes with a person's checkbook, and I'll tell you where their heart is." So, this is how it works, first you believe and confess your belief in Jesus Christ. And then, if you've truly rendered over your heart to God, you will begin to do good works by the giving of your time, talent, and money to the Kingdom of God and managing the resources that God gave you!

Now some of you may be asking yourself, "Isn't that a works-based salvation?" The answer is no. It's a heart-based salvation! Paul makes it clear in Romans 10:9 that we are saved by grace alone when he says, *'That if you confess with your mouth, "Jesus is Lord," and believe in your heart that God raised him from the dead, you will be saved.'* So, the question is, how do we know where someone's heart is? The simple answer is by their "fruit" or in other words, by their good works. James makes this clear when in the second chapter he asks the question, *"What good is it, my brothers, if a man claims to have faith but has no deeds? Can such faith save him?"* He goes on to answer the question with a resounding "NO"!!! Faith without works is dead.

Now, let's talk practicalities. While I don't know, and neither does Bryan, what each of us give, it doesn't take a math major to realize that we are not a tithing church. Some of us are new Christians that aren't familiar with the concept of tithing. Some of us are new Christians who have brought a challenging financial situation with them or who have made financial decisions that didn't take tithing into account. And some of us are lifelong Christians who have not been faithful to God and Jesus' call to give and there is a myriad of reasons why that is. Now, I'm not making a judgment call on this, it's just a fact and a fact that is not uncommon within any Church. As I said previously, tithing in and of itself is not a requirement for salvation. But it is a worthy goal. Can you image the additional good that this little church could do if every regular attendee gave a full 10% or more? The additional people we could reach, the additional money we could give to the poor among us, and the additional mission work we could accomplish. What a goal!

Now, some of you may be thinking to yourself, "is tithing a percentage of my check that I bring home after taxes or is it my gross pay?" I will let you know that Bryan and I differ on this but since I'm the one giving this talk, I'm going to tell you what I think. Here goes…God makes it clear in 1 Samuel 8:9 that government is inherently evil and warns his people to be careful about what they wish for. In addition, the First Commandment is "thou shall have no other gods before me". Based on all of this, you have to ask yourself, do you want to give your first fruits to the government, an organization that God's word tells us is inherently evil which our founding fathers knew firsthand. And aren't you in effect putting another god before God. A god who supposedly helps the poor by enabling poor choices and perpetuating a cycle of poverty. A god who squanders untold billions of dollars. Additionally, if you make say, $50,000 a year and you pay $10,000 in taxes, then the church only gets $4,000 (10% of $40,000). But if you tithe off the full amount you are giving $5,000 to the church and paying taxes on $45,000. Remember, Jesus said, *"Give unto Caesar what is Caesar's and give unto God what is God's"*. I don't know about you, but when it comes to giving, I'll be putting God first and everything else in its rightful position.

In three weeks, you will all be asked to make a pledge. The reason we need you to pledge is so we can set a budget and be able to set responsible spending guidelines for the operations of the church, for evangelism, and for mission work so that we can continue to be a 21st century expression of the 1st century church by being an authentic family of religious seekers and Christian believers who worship God together, grow in relationship with God and each other, serve in God's Kingdom together, give to God's Kingdom together, and invite others to do the same. Some of you may recognize that last part as the Morse Church's Mission Statement. A mission statement that I think truly exemplifies this church and I hope all of you will embrace it by making a pledge.

One last point I'd like to make about tithing. Notice that several times I said, "tithing of your time, talents, and money." So, what does tithing your time and talents look like? Well, there are 168 hours in a week which would mean giving seventeen hours a week to God in the form of worship, study, small groups, and serving others. Now if we were just talking about waking hours it was be about eleven hours. I just wanted to throw that out there so you can think about that over the next few days. I first heard this concept a few days ago myself and am still processing it.

Now, getting back to the financial pledge. If you're not able to pledge a full 10% of your income for whatever reason, please consider making your pledge a percentage of your income, whether it be 1% or 9% with the goal of working towards a full 10% or more when you're able. By making it a percentage of your income whatever that percentage may be, you are at least giving your "first fruits" to further God's kingdom.

Let me finish with a passage from Malachi; it's known as the Malachi Challenge. Malachi 3:10 says, *"Bring the whole tithe into the storehouse, that there may be food in my house. Test me in this," says the LORD Almighty, "and see if I will not throw open the floodgates of heaven and pour out so much blessing that there will not be room enough to store it."* Just think how much better the world would be and how much we would benefit the Kingdom of God if all believers tithed! And more importantly, think of the peace you will have knowing that you put God and His Kingdom first.

Amen.

God's Politics - Revisited

This is a talk that I am really dreading because I know that I'm going to make some people mad. Also, trying to narrow this talk down and organize my thoughts and not chasing multiple rabbit trails…well, let's just say it taxed my remaining gray matter to its limit, so let's get going.

Bryan has asked me to give this talk a couple of times over the years, but it wasn't until recently with all the turmoil that's been going on that I decided to give it. Actually, I had already had a large portion of it written when Bryan asked again last month.

The topic I'm giving today is God and Politics. Now, there is some irony here as both Bryan and I are obviously Christians and have very similar theological beliefs, but Bryan tends to vote for liberal democrats, and I tend to vote for conservative republicans. Because of this and the fact that many pastors are liberals, I began to question my political beliefs a couple of years ago. Although, I never told anyone, I began to doubt whether it was appropriate, as a Christian, to hold my political beliefs, and I was open to changing them if, biblically, it was appropriate. Although, I can be opinionated at times, I like to think that I'm a little open-minded. You can't go from atheism to belief in a creator and belief in Jesus without being a little open-minded. A little additional irony that I love to point out whenever I can (I probably beat a dead horse) but the secular (non-religious) community does a little projecting on Christians when they say we're narrow-minded bigots when, in fact, the vast majority of evidence points to a creator, and only blind adherence to their own dogma keeps them from seeing the truth. But I digress… So, I dug into the Bible to see what God had to say about politics and low and behold I did find out that my beliefs were wrong, and I have definitely changed my position on politics and how I vote (I'll get to that later).

Now, I had been mulling this for quite a while and really got jump started a couple months ago when Kathy and I, on our semi-annual date, were eating at the Blue Koi (you need to try the fried cheese cake - it'll change your life) and afterwards we walked around 39th Street and came across a used book store where I saw on the rack the book called "God's Politics: Why the Right Gets it Wrong and Why the Left Doesn't Get It." I had heard of this book, and it seemed to get good reviews which made me hope that it was an even-handed book that might shed some light on the subject. I was a little nervous, however, when I saw an endorsement by Bill Moyers on the jacket. I bought it anyway…who knows, Bill Moyers could've been right once in his life. Well anyway, I got through the first chapter which was a thinly veiled attack on our more fundamental brothers and a lamenting that our more liberal brothers (and atheist) don't get it, with the implication that they should get it because they're right about everything else. It was really a very disappointing book. Even as an untrained theologian like me, it was very easy to see that this book was a perfect example of eisegesis—that we read into scripture our own biases, in other words, taking passages out of context to fit your own predetermined outcome.

It was, however, after reading this first chapter that I realized that the book and most of the talks I've heard on God and politics, made by either the left or the right, are based on a false premise. That premise being that God cares about politics or government. What I realized in this moment of epiphany is that politics and governments are a creation of man and not of God. By allowing governments to exist, He has in essence ordained them, but that certainly doesn't mean that he approves of or controls them, although he has used them for His purposes. He also ordained the institution of marriage, but he doesn't pick our spouses. He tells us what we should look for in a spouse, but it is our decision. As with all things, we have free will to make judgments and decisions; let's just hope that we make those decisions based on scripture.

So, let's see what scripture says about governments. Let's go to the beginning with the Old Testament, or Torah, and start out with the first reference that I came across located in 1st Samuel, Chapter 8:4-18:

So, all the elders of Israel gathered together and came to Samuel at Ramah. They said to him, "You are old, and your sons do not walk in your ways; now appoint a king to lead us, such as all the other nations have."

But when they said, "Give us a king to lead us," this displeased Samuel; so he prayed to the LORD. And the LORD told him: "Listen to all that the people are saying to you; **it is not you they have rejected, but they have rejected me as their king** *(emphasis added). As they have done from the day I brought them up out of Egypt until this day, forsaking me and serving other gods, so they are doing to you. Now listen to them; but warn them solemnly and let them know what the king who will reign over them will do."*

Samuel told all the words of the LORD to the people who were asking him for a king. He said, "This is what the king who will reign over you will do: He will take your sons and make them serve with his chariots and horses, and they will run in front of his chariots. Some he will assign to be commanders of thousands and commanders of fifties, and others to plow his ground and reap his harvest, and still others to make weapons of war and equipment for his chariots. He will take your daughters to be perfumers and cooks and bakers. He will take the best of your fields and vineyards and olive groves and give them to his attendants. He will take a tenth of your grain and of your vintage and give it to his officials and attendants. Your menservants and maidservants and the best of your cattle and donkeys he will take for his own use. He will take a tenth of your flocks, and **you yourselves will become his slaves.**

(Emphasis added) When that day comes, you will cry out for relief from the king you have chosen, and the LORD will not answer you in that day."

Let's go back to verse 7. **"It is not you they have rejected, but they have rejected me as their king"**. So, God sees governments as a rejection of his authority, but he allowed it to happen only after letting the people know the consequences of their choice culminating with *"and you your-selves will become slaves"*. Since God is omniscient, he told his people the eventual outcome of any government, whether it is a monarchy, oligarchy, democracy, republic etc.; that outcome being tyranny and oppression.... **"and you yourselves will become his slaves."** All you have to look at is Solomon's reign, as he was big-time oppressor. In order to amass his great wealth and build the monuments he built, he did exactly what God had pre-dicted. Even the "wisest man" alive was corrupted by power and oppressed his people. When he died, his son (Rehoboam) had a choice to make; ease up on his subjects or continue on with the oppression. He chose to con-tinue to oppress and consequently lost his kingdom as he should have. So, we know that God doesn't like governments and see them as an affront to his authority and that if you choose to go with a government as your leader, you will face oppression *and* he will not help you get out of the mess you've gotten into! I think verse 18 is very interesting. *"When that day comes, you will cry out for relief from the king you have chosen, and the LORD will not answer you in that day."* As it relates to governments, God believes in the saying, "You've made your bed, now sleep in it."

So, let's see what Jesus had to say about governments. Jesus, at best, was indifferent towards governments. He could care less, and is this sur-prising since he said, *"If you know me, you know my father"*? He proved this when he made is famous entrance into Jerusalem on Palm Sunday. If you know the significance of the palms, you know that the people were escort-ing Jesus in as their Conquering Messiah. They wanted him to drive the Romans out of Israel and become their new king—their new earthly king. The palms represented a nationalistic symbol of the Jews and were a direct affront to the Romans and Caesar. But Jesus had nothing to do with this. As he would later tell Pilate, *"My kingdom is not of this world."*

Earlier, Jesus had told the Pharisees to give to Caesar the things that are Caesar's and give to God the things that are God's. The Pharisees were trying to trap Him into denouncing Rome as if he cared about human institutions. He surprised them with his indifference by saying, *"Give unto Caesar what is Caesar's, and give unto God what is God's."* So, this saying of Jesus begs the questions; what is God's role and what is government's role? Biblically, government's role is to protect it citizenry from foreign invaders and to mete out justice. The Church and the Christian's role is to love the Lord God with all your heart, soul, and mind, and to love your neighbors as yourself. Nowhere in the bible is there the concept of government helping any group by taking from one group and giving it to another. Government is supposed to refrain from making laws that oppress and withhold justice from the poor, or any of its citizens regardless of their economic position. *"Woe to those who make unjust laws, to those who issue oppressive decrees,"* as Isaiah 10:1 says. Justice is blind biblically as Leviticus 19:15 points out, *"Do not pervert justice: do not show partiality to the poor or favoritism to the great, but judge your neighbor fairly."* Any law or tax that benefits one group over another, shows partiality and is biblically unjust.

Now, I want to chase a small rabbit trail here to clear up an urban legend, or I should say a medieval legend: *Robin Hood.* Ever since I can remember, it was said that Robin Hood stole from the rich and gave to the poor. Whoever started that saying either didn't read the book or was a politician because Robin Hood stole from a confiscatory taxing authority, the Sheriff of Nottingham, and gave those taxes back to the people who were being oppressed by the government which was taxing its citizenry into poverty. Okay, back to it.

I'll use this as a segue into the modern concept of "Social Justice", that equality of outcome, as opposed to equality under the law, is the purpose of government. But, this is completely unbiblical and harms the Kingdom of God. First, the Bible teaches that you reap what you sow and that if you don't work you don't eat. That doesn't mean we are not supposed to help those less fortunate than us, but we are also not supposed to enable unproductive lifestyles and choices. Just a quick reading of proverbs shows that man needs to work and provide for himself and his family. As the Bible clearly illustrates, mercy without accountability is unjust enabling. In just about every circumstance where Jesus healed someone or showed mercy, he would say, *"go and sin no more."* Yet, there is no accountability in socialism. Accountability is counterproductive to dependency.

But worse yet, this idea of Social Justice oppresses all people in a society and makes people dependent on the government and creates an unsustainable cycle of greater and greater dependency. And, **this is the key**, this harms the kingdom of God by leading people away from God and making them dependent on the government thereby creating a competing god or idol, not only for those who are on the receiving end but also those who now think that they fulfilled their God given duty to help the needy by subordinating this duty to the government.

Let's look at welfare payments to the poor. It is estimated that twenty cents on the dollar go to the poor. Where does the other eighty cents go? To bureaucrats who are now dependent on government for their livelihood. And the number of bureaucrats increases every year causing more and more direct dependency on the government. And what about corporate welfare? Many industries are subsidized by the government which also creates dependency for those corporations, their employees, and the bureaucrats that administer those payments. ***"Do not pervert justice: do not show partiality to the poor or favoritism to the great, but judge your neighbor fairly." "He will take the best of your fields and vineyards and olive groves and give them to his attendants."***

By contrast, let's look at the Salvation Army. They give over 90% of the money they take in to the needy AND they show them and teach them about the love of God.

Now I said that this harms the Kingdom of God, so, why is this concept of Social Justice or Socialism so prevalent? It is just a modern repackaging of socialist and communistic ideals of the 19th century and secular progressive movement of the 20th century which in turn are based on atheistic ideals. They believe that since God doesn't exist that it is the role of government to be the supreme authority over people. That government must supplant God before utopia can exist. They believe the inevitable purpose of history is to *progress* to a utopian state. But remember, Jesus said, **"You will always have the poor among you,"** so the concept of a utopian state is not achievable and denies human nature.

Both Socialism and Communism came out of this school of thought that government must be the supreme authority which is only achievable if government assumes the role of god. That is why Darwin's Theory of Evolution was so uncritically accepted by atheist intellectuals of the time because it was so visual that the masses could readily understand it and "prove" that there is no need for a God thereby achieving one of their goals, the elimination of God. But one of many problems with atheistic evolutionary (in particular, macro evolution) thinking is what do you do with the poor and minorities or I should say, those who they consider to be less evolved than the intellectual elites who see themselves as higher on the evolutionary scale and now as the arbiters of right and wrong. There are only two options, eliminate them or become paternalistic towards them. The former option is the history of the early progressive movement of the 20th century in Europe and America. Hitler was a proponent of this. The first progressive President of the United States, Woodrow Wilson, reinstituted segregation in the government. Margaret Sanger was a progressive and she was for the forced sterilization of the poor and minorities. That is why she started Planned Parenthood. Have you ever noticed that almost all Planned Parenthood clinics are in predominately poor and minority locations? This is not by accident. And the black community is finally coming to realize this. Black pastors are finally speaking out. There is an excellent documentary called Maafa 21 which is a documentary on the genocide of blacks that has taken place right under our noses.[3] The other option, paternalism, is where the government must rule over and protect the poor because they're not *"evolved"* enough or *enlightened enough* to rule over themselves. Under this form, a centralized planning apparatus is needed to run our lives. Communism, Socialism, social democracies, and fascism are examples of this. The dirty little secret is that sometimes individuals don't like what the government says is best for them so that have to be dealt with. That is why Stalin murdered 30 million of his citizen and Mao is said to have murdered up to 70 million of his citizens. So, it's very easy for paternalistic societies to revert to option number one, genocide.

As Thomas Jefferson said, "Government big enough to supply everything you need is big enough to take everything you have." While we're at it, let's clear up another modern urban legend. Prior to 1945, Jefferson's quote to the Danbury Baptists (the "wall of separation" quote) was used by the courts as it was intended; to keep government out of the affairs of the Church, **not** to keep religion out of government as it is now used by secular progressives and worldly Christians. This goes totally against Jefferson's intent and practice as he and the other founding fathers saw the need, and provided for, religion within government as an additional check and balance. They knew that government (as the Bible and history showed them), any government, could not exist without the three-legged stool that I heard described by Christian Philosopher Os Guinness: "Liberty requires virtue, virtue requires religion." What we are seeing now in society is one leg of that stool being removed, religion. Without it, the stool topples and so does our society. Our government needs religion to survive but religion, or I should say Christian faith, doesn't need government to survive. The Bible and history are replete with examples of this. Governments are formed following God; the people move away from God and governments topple;

---

3 Planned Parenthood is the most evil organization ever devised in the history of the world. Since Roe v. Wade, almost 62 million babies have been aborted in the U.S. alone. Of these abortions, 29% were black babies. Blacks only make up 12.4% of the total US population. It looks like Margaret has partially fulfilled her objective. By the way, even as an atheist, I was against abortions. It seemed sick and wrong, but I didn't realize at the time that this view was inconsistent with my atheist beliefs.

people come back to God and the cycle continues. Human nature doesn't change - it never evolves!

Okay, let's bring this out of the theoretical and into the present. Let's face it. The secular progressives have won the battle. The only question is will they win the war? Europe is now a fully secularized society. In America, also, the battle is almost over. Secular ideas are taught in our schools and universities as fact. The culture has been nearly fully secularized. The secular progressives have been allowed to remove religion from the public square to a large degree. Worst yet, many churches have adopted the idea of social justice and working within the government to achieve it, doing so in direct conflict to biblical principles. The irony is that secular progressive know that biblical Christianity is completely incompatible with their goals and fight for its destruction, but many Christians and Christian institutions think they can adopt these ideals and not harm the Kingdom of God in much the same way they adopted evolution. I recently read a study that compared spending on social programs in societies to the level of Christianity. What the authors found is a direct correlation to social spending and the level of Christianity. As social spending increases, the level of Christianity decreases. This confirms that these atheistic ideals are not compatible with Christianity and to accept them only pits you against God. And what I find funny is that none of this new information. Some of you may think that I'm partaking in a grand conspiracy theory, but this information and the intent of the secular progressive movement has been around for years and most of it written by them. I recently read the Brothers Karamazov written by Dostoyevsky, said by Freud and Einstein as one of the greatest novels ever written. This book was written in the 1880s and explores many of these ideas and even then, realizes the consequences of atheism.

It's only because Christian institutions have chosen to ignore this threat, and actually enable it by voting for people who promote it, simply because they market it under the guise of "helping the poor, or helping the sick, or helping the elderly." I mean, who's against any of those things? They are Christian values! The problem is that most Christians no longer follow the biblical principle of testing "spirits" against scripture and are caught up in emotionalism. What is a spirit? It can simply be an emotion or feeling that comes over you that leads you to make a decision. So, when someone says, "they want to help the poor", emotionally we react to that in a positive way. But is that a spirit from God or is it coming from somewhere else? That's why it needs to be tested against scripture to see its origin. So, let's test "helping the poor." Are we to help the poor? Sure, we are. Are we supposed to take property from someone against their will and give to someone else? Of course not—*"thou shall not steal."* Doing this shows partiality which in turn leads to one group resenting the other, and one group coveting what the other group has—*"thou shall not covet."* So, governmental social justice fails miserably when tested against scripture. The problem is that Christians have become undiscerning and let their emotions rule their decisions and not biblical principles—I'm as guilty of this as anyone!

We are almost to the anniversary of the last presidential election. So, how should we as Christian's vote. First, we should never put a political party above God. That is why I am no longer a Republican. I realized that I was self-identifying as a Republican and not as a Christian and voting for people just because they were Republicans. I will only register for a party in order to vote in a primary for the right candidate. Second, we should never vote for a candidate that will enact laws that will harm the Kingdom of God. I can tell you without a doubt that as a Christian, I would vote differently this time. I voted for John McCain even though I didn't like many of his policies, but I felt he was the lesser of two evils. But if you vote for the lesser of two evils, what are you guaranteed to get? Evil. You just get it a little slower. Today I wouldn't vote for either candidate. Both have aligned themselves with the secular progressive movement, McCain certainly to a lesser extent, but both will increase government's paternalistic control over you, and I refuse to vote for anyone who will fight against God. I won't do it. *"But Gib, you have to vote."* No, you don't. I'll register to vote, and I'll vote for candidates that will promote the Kingdom of God and if there are none, then so be it. As a Christian, I can no longer do it.

Now, both candidates for president claimed to be Christians. So, do we as Christians just vote for Christians? The answer is "no". If someone has views that align with and benefit the Kingdom of God, I'll vote for them regardless of their religion. Throughout history, God has used people of other religions to His benefit. God used Cyrus, the King of Persia, for example, to end the Babylonian captivity of the Jews (confirmed by archaeology) and let them return to Jerusalem.

As far as the current debate about health care reform, I'm all for it. The health care industry is one of the most highly regulated industries there is which is the reason why it's so expensive. The best thing that could happen to the poor and elderly is for Medicaid and Medicare to go away and for the government to get out of healthcare. If they did this, the church would step in and fill the void, providing better, more efficient care and showing the love of God. All you have to do is look at what happened with Katrina. The government utterly failed, and it was the church that came in and took up the slack and is still down there today helping to rebuild.

But, Gib, you have to vote, or it'll just get worse. Yes, it may. But sometimes things have to get worse before they get better. Besides, if Christians continue to vote for politicians who harm the kingdom of God, then there is absolutely no reason for them to change. They will continue doing what they're doing without any regard for God's will and why should they— Christians vote them in. And if you think God is going to intervene on our behalf, I'll refer back to verse 18, *"When that day comes, you will cry out for relief from the king you have chosen, and the LORD will not answer you in that day."* We as Americans think that our country has free pass as it relates to God just because we were founded on biblical principles. But we don't. God didn't give Israel or Judah a pass when they decided to turn away from God and we have certainly turned away from God as a country. Really, you don't have to be a prophet to see that as a country we only have two options (aside from Jesus returning, which of course is by far the best option): we continue on the path that we're on and there is either a revolt or we implode as a country, or there is biblical revival. Notice I didn't say a spiritual revival. The church over the last hundred years has been in a spiritual phase which is why the church is in the state that it is currently in. Let me explain, when you have just spiritualism it leads to mysticism, or worse Gnosticism, which simply is "if you just believe, secret knowledge will be made known to you." This heresy was identified by the first century church and dealt with. When you have truth only, you have legalism as was the situation with the Pharisees during the time of Jesus. It's only when spirit and truth work together that the Church explodes, and you have a true revival as in Great Awakening. As John Wesley said,

"Unite the pair so long disjoined,

Knowledge and vital piety

Learning and holiness combined,

And truth and love let all men see."

But the best example of this is the early Church. Jesus' resurrection proved that He was God. This truth combined with the Holy Spirit exploded the church like nothing ever seen in history. Jesus himself said in John 4:23, *"Yet a time is coming when the true worshipers will worship the father in spirit and truth, for they are the kind of worshipers the Father seeks."*

So, the *only* hope for the country is for the Church and Christians to come back to biblical principles. So, Christians need to educate themselves in the undeniable facts that are the foundation of their faith *and* engage in the electoral process by informing your friends and neighbors of these issues and supporting candidates who will govern by biblical principles because whatever is good for the Church is good for the country!

I'll finish with a quote Hosea 8:4: "*They set up kings without my consent; they choose princes without my approval. With their silver and gold, they made idols for their own destruction.*"

What Does it Mean to Believe?

"To be or not to be? That is the question I ask of thee."
- Gilligan, *Gilligan's Island*

Gilligan's rendition of Hamlet's soliloquy set to Carmen's Habenera is anything but a great stage performance. But it does ask the correct question, to be or not to be, or for the purposes of these final thoughts, belief or non-belief—that is the question?

According to Oxford Dictionary, belief means *"something one accepts as true or real; a firmly held opinion or conviction."* According to this definition, beliefs can be either rational or irrational. I would suggest that many people in the western world think that belief in Jesus, or any religion, is irrational; that religions by their very nature cannot be proven and therefore it takes faith (irrational faith) to believe in them.

But, here's the irony, non-belief (call it atheism or agnosticism) is a belief system; a religion. Because, even if people don't think that they believe in the supernatural, this in itself is a "belief" because they can't be certain that there isn't a God. Even Richard Dawkins, the high priest of atheism, admits that there is a chance that there is a God, however slight.

Now, if you know the definition of atheism, this self-proclaimed atheist is a wee bit confused since he just admitted he is an agnostic (someone who thinks that if there is a god that it is unknowable) and not an atheist.

Now Dawkins, along with most atheists and agnostics, think they are rational agents—more rational that the knuckle-dragging religious types. But…wait, wait…atheism, as I said, is a religion and an irrational one at that. In order to believe that we were not created and that there is no God, first, they must be all-knowing—let me explain. It is much easier to prove that something "exists" as opposed to something "not existing." I'll steal an analogy that heard several years ago to show you what I mean. Let's assume you say, "There are no black cats in Olathe". To prove this wrong, all we need do is find a black cat. To prove it correct, we have to round up all the cats in Olathe to ensure that there are no black cats. Now extrapolate to black cats in the United States or in the world and you'll see where the problem lies. To say that there is no God, you need to have all of the knowledge of the universe to positively confirm this. And if there is a God who exists outside of universe (hence, the word "supernatural"), you would also have to know what is outside of our universe. In order to prove that there is a God, all you would need is one piece of evidence (Jesus' resurrection, the fine tuning of the universe, weak/strong atomic force, design in nature, fulfilled Bible prophecy, on and on…). The evidences for God are many and convincing—beyond a reasonable doubt.

Now further, to believe in atheism, you must have the very non-scientific belief that "something came from nothing". Actually, you have to believe this twice. First, you must believe that the universe, us in effect, came from nothing. That at some point in the distant past, there was nothing. There is no getting around it. Philosophers throughout history, Christian and non-Christian—Plato, for example—have understood that for us to exist today, something has to be eternal, either the universe or something outside the universe. Since the evidence for the Big Bang is overwhelming, we know that the universe had a beginning, so we know something outside of the universe must be uncreated and always self-existing. Now, as finite beings, this is a mind-blowing concept, but since we know that all space, time, and matter (material) in the universe started at the Big Bang, we know that whatever being created the Big Bang, that that being must be all powerful, immaterial, and timeless which is the description of God in the Bible. Despite all their attempts to explain this away, atheists still have no feasible alternative to this other than non-provable, esoteric theories that rely on infinite regression, so it takes a lot of irrational faith to believe in atheism.

The other "something from nothing" that they believe, is that information just happened by itself. Let's think about this. DNA, which, even in the simplest of organism, contains a mindboggling amount of information. As Bill Gates, the founder of Microsoft, said, "DNA is like a computer program but far, far more advanced than any software we've ever devised." Where did this information come from? Now for years, naturalist will have you believe that the primordial ooze produced amino acids that formed proteins, and these proteins then folded themselves into the DNA molecule and then, voila, with the information receptacle in place, information appeared that is able to design and manufacture the first organism complete with a microscopic factory that is able to deliver, refine, transport the refined product and waste materials, then dispose of the waste material, and most amazingly, replicate itself. You don't have the intelligence of a Mensa member to know that it takes a lot of information to pull this off, and it has to be functional information—information that has a purpose.

So, where did the information come from? We know from our world around us, that functional information, information with a purpose, needs intelligence to produce it—it just doesn't happen on its own regardless of the amount of time. Prior to life on earth, it was just inorganic dirt with no intelligence and no means of producing functional information. So, again saying that an information-less world produced information is saying that you can get something from nothing, which is why Antony Flew, one of the most famous atheists in the 20th century, changed his tune. As he said later in life, *"Super-intelligence is the only good explanation for the origin of life and the complexity of nature."*

So, you see that atheism is an irrational belief system that fits a definition of religion, "a cause, principle, or system of beliefs held with ardor and faith". Just like other religions, they have dogmas (strict adherence to naturalism), fundamentalist (the New Atheists), high priests (Richard Dawkins, Sam Harris, etc.), and a holy book (Darwin's, *On the Origin of the Species*). One thing they have done better than all other religions, they have painted themselves as the only rational belief system, and not a belief system at all—they are just following the "truth". It is very deceptive and attractive; you get to feel superior to others, and you are in essences your own god as you get to determine your own truth (postmodernism). It personifies the phrase, "if it feels good, do it", something that most adults know, post-puberty, isn't workable long-term.

In addition to the atheist, there is a large and growing segment of the population that are known as "Nones" as they have no religious affiliation. Some are spiritual but don't want anything to do with organized religion and some just don't care; it is a non-factor in their lives. In addition to the Nones, there are those who call themselves Christians but don't follow Christ in any meaningful way. All of these groups, including agnostics, are functional atheist. While they are living off the Christian heritage of their forefathers, life is all about self-actualization, an atheist concept, and not about self-sacrifice, a biblical concept.

So, the point of all of this is that regardless of what group you identify with, you are part of a belief system (or religion) whether like it or not. As I'm sure you are now aware, I believe in Christ because it is the only rational option, the only option that is supported by clear and convincing evidence.

So, since Christianity is the only rational choice, what does it mean to truly believe in Jesus?

The Apostle Paul says in Romans 10:9, *"If you confess with your mouth that Christ is Lord, and you believe in your heart that He was raised from the dead, you will be saved."* This really sounds too easy. It certainly isn't hard to believe he was raised from the dead as there is ample evidence, both direct and circumstantial, for this historical fact. Philosophically, it also easy to believe. By way of analogy, if a mechanic and body shop can bring a car "back to life" after an accident, I don't think it would be too hard for the Creator of the universe to bring His son back to life.

The first part of Paul's statement, "if you confess with mouth that Christ is Lord", at first blush seem easy also, and it certainly can be, if you make Christ your "Lord". But what does lord mean? According to Merriam-Webster a "lord" means: "a ruler by hereditary right or preeminence to whom service and obedience are due." So, we are supposed to serve and give obedience to Jesus. What does this look like? I'll let Jesus tell you. First, Jesus says, *"If you love me, obey my commands" (John 14:15)*. Further Jesus says, *"Love the Lord your God with all your heart and with all your soul and with all your mind. This is the first and greatest commandment. And the second is like it: 'Love your neighbor as yourself.' All the Law and the Prophets hang on these two commandments" (Matthew 22:37-40)*. And finally, Jesus said, *"So in everything, do to others what you would have them do to you, for this sums up the Law and the Prophets" (Matthew 7:12- The Golden Rule)*. So, in order to follow Jesus and have him be your "Lord", in the very simplest terms, you have to obey Jesus and treat people the way you want to be treated.

Now, as a point of clarification, none of this must be done *prior* to committing to Jesus and being saved. This is a free choice we all make, and we are not hindered by any of our actions prior to this commitment. As the Apostle Paul put it, *"For it is by grace you have been saved, through faith—and this is not from yourselves, it is the gift of God—not by works, so that no one can boast. For we are God's handiwork, created in Christ Jesus to do good works, which God prepared in advance for us to do." (Ephesians 2:10)*. So, Paul makes it very clear, it is a free gift from God, and it is up to us if we accept it. Once you believe that Jesus was raised from the dead and accept him as your Lord and Savior, it is up to us, with the help of the Holy Spirit, to obey Him and keep His commands by doing good (good works) with what we have been given. As the Apostle James said, *"What good is it, my brothers and sisters, if someone claims to have faith but has no deeds? Can such faith save them?" (James 2:14)*. Jesus himself points this out in the Parable of the Talents (Matthew 25:14-28), where one of the master's servants is chastised severely as he does nothing with the talent (gold) he is entrusted with while his master is away.

So, there you have it, belief in Christ is both rational and relational. Rational, in that it is backed up by evidence, and relational, in as we decide to follow Him, we are to obey Jesus' commands by loving God and loving our neighbors. As you read in the chapter on love, love is a verb of action and not a feeling.

Let me finish this up with Pascal's Wager, made famous by 17th century world-renown mathematician, physicist, and philosopher, Blaise Pascal. He argued that humans bet with their lives as to whether God exists or doesn't exist. If He exists, we have everything to gain (heaven and eternal life) and nothing to lose as religious people are happier (as several studies have shown), and more satisfied with their lives than non-religious people. Whereas, if we choose not to believe in God, then you have nothing to gain (your life is not improved) and everything to lose (eternal life in hell). While this philosophical argument doesn't prove or disprove that there is a God, it does make the argument that belief in God is at the very least is pragmatic. But, more importantly, this should encourage you to take an honest, open-minded look at evidence for God.

Now that I think about it, there is one last issue that needs to be discussed; what can you expect from the Christian life?

I have had significant financial success in my years compared to most in the world. Compared to the United States, I'm probably in the middle of the pack of successful people—success as measured by worldly standards. I've been fortunate enough to be able to buy things I want (not need), especially in the last few years. But I have realized that material success is fleeting and offers limited joy. Some people are fortunate enough to be born not needing "things", others learn this later in life, and others never do learn this. The Bible teaches this same principle about how "stuff" is unimportant, but we humans often have to learn things the hard way. I have found that giving things away and helping people regardless of what I get in return, provides much more joy and satisfaction than buying and obtaining "stuff". This is the "good works" the Bible talks about—helping and loving your neighbors.

It is good that God designed us this way because the Christian life can be challenging. Contrary to what the "Prosperity preachers" teach, God is not a cosmic slot machine that grants you your every heart's desire—and a Mercedes Benz (thank you, Janis Joplin). However, if you follow Biblical teachings of Jesus and those found in Proverbs, they are the best guide for living a successful, fulfilled life. There is another "however"—and this is a big one—*however*, Jesus makes it very clear that by becoming a Christian and following Him, while his "yoke is easy", your life may involve more conflict, not less. We here in the U.S. are very fortunate that as Christians, we don't not suffer persecution to the extent that it is found elsewhere in the world. But, with the secularization of America, that has changed very rapidly over the last twenty years. I certainly don't want to imply that the soft persecution that we now live with is anything compared to what is going on in some Muslim nations or China (or the east and west coasts), but it is out there, and you need to be aware of it. There are several biblical principles that elucidate this, but I recently read a book about religious freedom conflicts that did a far better job than I could have done, so I won't reinvent the wheel here. The book, *Free to Believe: The Battle Over Religious Liberty in America*, by Luke Goodrich, the author below tells how as Christians we are to react when the inevitable conflicts arise:

"Scripture, however, calls us to a radically different approach. We're called not to win but to be like Jesus; not to fear suffering but to fear God; not to be surprised at hostility but to expect it; not to complain when we lose but to rejoice; not to lash out at our opponents but to love them. We're called not to avoid losing at all costs but to glorify God at all costs."

First off, all the above principles violate human nature, so, how is it possible to following them? Those who know me best, know that I have not been true to these principles. I have not, and probably will not, live up to each and every one of these principles at all times. Even the apostles on occasion had to be reminded that they were acting inconsistent with Jesus' teachings—that is the human condition. What's instructive is that after Jesus' death and resurrection, and the apostles receiving the Holy Spirit, their lives exemplified these principles (with rare exemptions). As Jesus said, *"With man this is impossible, but with God all things are possible"* (Matthew 19:26).[4]

Okay, it's time to finally wrap this up. Christianity is harder than a life of self-satisfaction, but it is more satisfying. It is harder than a life of merriment, but you become merrier. But it is easier than a life of "keeping up with the Jones", because you'll be jones'n on Jesus! (I know that is corny). Let's try it this way; it is easier than a life chasing after the next big thing to bring relevance to your life because Christ has already made you relevant. Besides, living a lie never works but living following Truth is always rewarding regardless of the consequences. To rework a line from a Lyle Lovett song, "if I weren't [trying to be] the man [Jesus] wanted, I wouldn't be the man that I am."

---

4 Jesus says this after talking to the "rich young ruler" where he says, *"It is easier for camel to pass through the eye of a needle, than for someone who is rich to enter the kingdom of God."* The apostles were taken aback as the Sadducees and the Pharisees were the "rich" in that society because, as they and the people thought, they were the most religious and therefore received the most material blessings from God. So, if they couldn't enter God's kingdom (or earn their way into it), who could?

Postscript

So, if you're a Believer, I hope this book has answered some of your questions and encouraged you to become a BOC[5] if you're not one already. If you aren't a believer, I hope that I've piqued your interest enough that you'll study the evidence for God with an open mind. As I said in the Introduction, a mind open to Truth and mystery.

So, here are my parting words: as it relates to religion, I don't care what you think. If you can tell me *why* you think it, then *maybe* you have something. What you think only matters on subjective issues (and then it really only matters to you). If what you think can change reality (in other words, becomes your truth), then you are god… and you are not god!

Remember, "What you do in life, echoes in eternity"!

---

5 "Big 'Ole Christian" as my Friday morning men's group likes to call committed followers of Christ.